You can learn to ignore life's distractions

You can overcome fear and doubt

You can have intimacy with God

STATIC

JEDI™

THE ART OF HEARING **GOD**
THROUGH THE NOISE

ERIC SAMUEL TIMM
Foreword by **MARK BATTERSON**

Eric Samuel Timm's book, *Static Jedi*, is a refreshing reminder that God is always there ready to meet with us. You will be inspired and encouraged in your own personal pursuit of God. The simple truth is that we need to seek time with Him and life can sometimes get in the way. *Static Jedi* uses practical steps from Jesus's life to radically transform yours.

—MICHAEL W. SMITH
Singer/songwriter

Balancing six kids, a wonderful marriage, football, speaking, and my spiritual walk is never an easy undertaking. The pace of life can easily take over. In this hustle it's easy to find faith buried in the busy. *Static Jedi* is an excellent playbook for setting up followers of Christ for success in each play of life. Eric's unique and profoundly effective communication style is fully captured in written articulation on the pages of this book. It's creative, entertaining, and packed with profound meaning. Let it challenge you as you get centered. I'm thankful our lives have collided.

—MATT BIRK
Speaker and author
All-pro center, Baltimore Ravens Super Bowl XLVII champions

There are so many books today on how to help you manage what EST in this much-awaited book calls the "noise." I appreciate that this book is not about managing the noise but mastering it. Eric artfully explains that it is truly just noise, and once mastered, the reward is far greater.

—CRAIG GROSS
Founder, xxxchurch.com
Author, *Open: What Happens When You Get Real,
Get Honest and Get Accountable*

Static Jedi is the challenging reminder that I needed. I now have a renewed excitement to place my priorities in connecting with Christ in a more meaningful and focused manner. Not out of legalistic obligation but out of a deep desire to know and understand the heart of Christ. Eric's quirky sense of humor and relatable approach made *Static Jedi* an easy yet focused read that I did not want to put down till the final page was turned. Focusing on what matters and mastering the noise should be an aspiration for us all.

—GLENN DRENNEN
Member, award-winning rock band Fireflight

Eric Samuel Timm has used his artistic and communication gifts to transform the lives of millions of adults and students. I have often wondered how one person could be so talented. Now I discover he can also masterfully write. The stories in his first book, *Static Jedi*, are funny, heart grabbing and life changing. I'm jealous! I know it's wrong, but I'm still jealous! I'm also challenged. Read it; you won't put it down.

—KEN DAVIS
Best-selling author, inspirational speaker,
gifted comedian, master storyteller

God has formed in me a true heart for divine intimacy. Yet I seriously have a big problem mastering the noise. The traveling life of a rock star, along with my cell phone, iPad, and iPhone completely rob me of intimacy with Jesus. *Static Jedi* by EST fell into my lap at the perfect time. This book is an extremely important word for God's people at this moment in history. We need to seriously take this message to heart!

—BRIAN "HEAD" WELCH
Love and Death band, author, speaker,
and former guitarist for Korn

From the first interaction I had with Eric it was obvious he was one of the most creative and passionate and gifted communicators around. Again this is true with his recent work on *Static Jedi*. In a world full of noise I am thankful that Eric again draws us back to the clarion voice of God found in His Word. Give us ears to hear.

—J. ROGER DAVIS
President, Student Life

My friend Eric Samuel Timm has written a book that had me laughing out loud one minute and took me to the face of Jesus the next minute. This book reinvigorated my passion for the "perpetual discovery" of Jesus through giving Him more than just a time of devotion…and learning how to make every moment of my life a time of devotion. I am officially joining the Static Jedi Order.

—KEVIN YOUNG
Award-winning rock band Disciple

Weird title, awesome book. Quirky author, insightful thinker. Unique style, fresh ideas.

—MARK OESTREICHER
Partner, The Youth Cartel
Author

Eric Samuel Timm is a dynamic speaker and has challenged me in several areas of my own spiritual walk. I believe you will be both encouraged and challenged by what Eric says, and if we are willing to step out, God can use those challenges to help us draw closer to Him.

—JON MICAH SUMRALL
Award-winning rock band Kutless

Inspiration is one of the most powerful driving forces in the world. When Christians become inspired by the words and life of Christ, there is no limit to what God can do in and through them. *Static Jedi* sends an amazing message and challenge to believers to move past the noise and chaos of life into a place of deeper relationship with God. Read the book. Be encouraged. Most of all, be inspired.

—Jeremy Kingsley
President, One Life Leadership
Best-selling author, *Inspired People Produce Results*

I remember when the ability to multitask was a leader's pursuit: the more a leader could absorb and decipher, the better. Today's leadership climate demands something much more primal and simpler than that. Our ability to mono-task and hone in on the one voice that brings clarity and creativity amidst all of the noise will set us apart as a spouse, parent, student, or professional. Eric unearths one simple concept that can easily become complicated. He summons us to the profound elementary truth of fixing our eyes on the One who speaks, for it is here that we find all we need. This timely response and proactive approach is a gift to us all.

—Heath Adamson
National youth director, Assemblies of God

Intimacy with God is mastering the spiritual discipline of creating sacred space that is mobile. This is to cultivate community and harmony with the triune God not only when you sit but also when you move in the flow of life. *Static Jedi* is more than a resource on spiritual intimacy; this is a paradigm changer that will hydrate your soul unto spiritual renewal. Mastering the noise of the chaos of life is not only crucial but also life giving. Eric Samuel Timm is a minister to ministers, and these precepts are not only preached but also practiced in humility and servitude. I highly encourage you to read, glean, and position your heart to fight for godliness.

—Dr. Ed Newton
Bible communicator, Memphis, TN

Eric is one of the most creative people I know. Many have seen his masterful storytelling on the painted canvas. In *Static Jedi* Eric takes on a canvas—the written page—in order to sketch a portrait of a disciple of Jesus living today in a fresh and compelling way.

—SHANE STACEY
National director, ReachStudents
Evangelical Free Church of America

Any church would benefit from experiencing this book together. If you have ever found yourself overwhelmed, disconnected from God, and wading through the static of your day, you need to read this book. Eric expertly navigates this hard-to-master skill and lays out an easy road map that anyone can follow. After all, he takes his cues from Jesus's example in Scripture—what better model than that?

—ROB KETTERLING
Lead pastor, River Valley Church

In *Static Jedi* Eric tackles the issue of our noisy, distracted lives in a fresh and creative way…and if you know Eric, you know that's the only way he's going to address anything! Eric thinks differently, lives differently, and writes differently, which is why I'm constantly drawn to what he has to say. This book speaks with a broad brush that challenged me personally. I know it will challenge my students as well.

—KURT JOHNSTON
Pastor to students, Saddleback Church

Static Jedi is a timely book that challenges believers to move beyond the noise of this life to a place of unparalleled faith and closeness with God. It attacks, without defeat, mediocrity and complacency, the silent killers in the pursuit of God. The book, in a very practical way, draws you where you need to go in your faith. Let it move you, challenge you, and change you!

—Clayton King
Speaker and author
Campus pastor, Liberty University
Founder, Crossroads Worldwide

With a direct word from the Lord for this time, Eric jabs into the heart of what has potential to steal our hearts and offers practical knowledge as well as theory and mind-set for beginners and veterans of following Christ alike. An important tool for an important time in our spiritual history.

—Dave Decker Jr.
Pastor to creatives
Founder, LightsOut

Eric Samuel Timm masters the pen as well as the artist paintbrush. He is not just a hearer of the Word but also a doer of the Word. His latest body of work portrays his passion for the kingdom in the only way he can—by creating vivid landscapes of thought and reflection, challenge and action, humility and faith. There is something in *Static Jedi* for every reader who desires to find purpose and meaning out of life and to courageously navigate their way to the waiting, outstretched arms of Jesus. A must-read for the master in all of us. It's time to cut through the noise and get real with God.

—Blake Silverstrom
Director, OneHope

Eric has captured the essence of a passion and commitment to Christ. In *Static Jedi* you'll be inspired and encouraged to further your pursuit of God, to deepen your commitment to Christ, and to make Christ known in a "noisy" world full of distractions.

The real-life application in each chapter will compel you to think internally as well as externally.

—JEFF PIEPER
Alliance director, Luis Palau Association

Eric Samuel Timm's *Static Jedi* is an inspiration not only to simplify one's life but also to make more of the time we are given. It is a guide on how to bridle life's noise and use it for a greater purpose rather than be overwhelmed by it. As a musician and artist, it reminds me that to be who I really was created to be, I must be still and listen to the Creator. Out of that comes God's vision for my creativity—God's songs for my life of worship. My prayer is to quiet my noise to hear God's clarity.

—JACOB OLDS
Member, award-winning rock band Family Force 5

From his heart as an artist, Eric Samuel Timm uses a pen this time instead of a brush! He has painted in words a pointed challenge of the noise, craziness, and busyness in our lives. He uses some deep colors to convict and call us to more, or is it to less? It's both. Less noise. More stillness.

—BOB LENZ
Life Promotions
International speaker and author

Eric sheds so much light on the dark situation we all have put ourselves into that it hurts, and I'm glad it hurts. A broken generation needs tools provided in *Static Jedi* to even realize how broken we are. His creative insight into finding true emotional and spiritual balance is a must "read and do book" for all of us!

—SCOTT BRINSON
Founder, My Broken Palace

I've known EST for nearly ten years for his brilliant brush strokes on blank canvases. In *Static Jedi* he has painted a masterpiece for this generation with his words. Every Christian should be armed with the truths and wisdom Eric has packed in this book. Turn off the noise and start reading now!

—TERRY WEAVER
Speaker and author, *Making Elephants Fly*
Editor, "Capture"

I would especially recommend this book for couples and families who are crippled by busyness. Read it together to recenter, refocus, and reengage with God and each other! Eric's healthy, tell-it-like-it-is approach is fun, meaningful, and spiritually practical.

—AARON GONYOU
Director, marketing and communications
Compassion Canada

Eric Samuel Timm is the most creative communicator I know. He is a deep well in the Word who is inspiring and challenging. *Static Jedi* is a must-read. I dare you!

—RANDY YOUNG
Relations manager to artists, speakers, and events
World Vision Canada

When I meet Eric, I was riveted by his creativity as well as his clarity in presenting a life-changing message that informed as well as educated the listener. In *Static Jedi* Eric again communicates timeless truth in a way that engages the reader as well as challenges common opinion. Eric has nailed, in a creative way, the passion of the lost. This is a must-read.

—JOHN MAY
District youth director, Potomac Youth Network

Eric's writing style captures you immediately, and the revelation God drops through him in this book is revelatory. The book was so convicting, it sparked kitchen table conversation and tears while I read it.

—JORGE AND KAT VAZQUEZ
The Revolution TV

Eric Samuel Timm is one of the most creative people I have ever met. On and off the stage he wows people with his wit, humor, and artistry. In *Static Jedi* once again he doesn't fail to bring us to the edge of our seats and show us a new horizon over cliffs we could not previously see, into the art that is God Himself. While he teaches you to be a static Jedi and master the noise of your life in this book, you feel you are in a different sound wave all together.

—MATT BROWN
Evangelist and author
Founder, Think Eternity

Eric has demonstrated time and again his ability to hear from God, then clearly communicate a relevant and timely message. His passion and unique style have made him a favorite of both students and leaders. The message of *Static Jedi* will both challenge and equip each reader to overcome the noise that holds them back from their potential. You will be challenged to live at a place you've not yet reached.

—MARK DEAN
Director, Minnesota Youth Ministries

Pushing gravity and testing limits, life is an awesome adventure! Experiencing life to the full is what Jesus offers. *Static Jedi* challenges you to get more than you ever thought you could out of your relationship with Jesus by taking your faith past the point it is today. Live life in rarefied air. Read the book and begin the truest adventure!

—MARIO D'ORTENZIO
Founder/director, Death 2 Life Revolution

Eric Samuel Timm is one of the most talented and creative people I know, and he uses unique communication skills to effectively identify the many distractions that will drown out the life-giving voice of God. This book will renew one's desire to hear the Lord's voice while offering practical solutions to illuminate the distractions that lure us away daily.

—RICHARD CRISCO
President, Empowering Kingdom Leaders
International speaker and author
Pastor, Rochester First Assembly, Michigan

Every chapter produces fruit on this subject and has one takeaway statement/illustration that has to be highlighted, journaled, tweeted, or retold in person. A good book contains scriptures. A great book points you back to discover even more in the Scriptures. *Static Jedi* is that kind of book; EST is that kind of author.

—JONNY MAC
Pastor of students, Southeast Christian Church
Louisville, Kentucky

Eric Samuel Timm isn't only one of the funniest and most creative human beings I know, but he has also written works that speak to the soul in his book, *Static Jedi*. My life is surrounded by noise, and often I miss the message God is trying to relay because of the noise. I appreciate this book, and I look forward to the response the world has when they read these words.

—MATT BAIRD
Lead singer award-winning rock band Spoken

Static Jedi is a must-read for all who are serious about living a life of true peace. The words are Eric's paint, every sentence is filled with gripping color. He has turned his pen into a brush and the pages into canvas. Read it only if you want to be moved to change the volume of God's love in your life.

—SAM FARNIA
Evangelist, author, pastor

I'm impressed with Eric's genuine call and artistic approach to sharing the gospel of Jesus outside of this book. However, inside this book Eric encourages you to not live in the static of life. Instead he challenges you to make every moment count and follow Jesus with total abandon to self. It will also make you smile a lot and write out witty quotes on Facebook.

—TIM BYRNE
Pro skateboarder, evangelist

I'm so glad Eric is addressing this issue of noise and distraction in our culture today. It is the battle of our generation. In *Static Jedi* I believe you will find practical and helpful advice on how to follow and pursue Jesus in the midst of changing crazy times.

—KRISTIAN STANDFILL
Award-winning recording artist

Read *Static Jedi* and you'll experience Eric Samuel Timm dropping some Jesus power on you, Obi-Wan Kenobi style! But the force you'll get isn't fictional; it's authentic Holy Spirit power helping you master the noisy gauntlet of life choices. Read this book!

—TONY NOLAN
Gospel preacher, @tonynolanlive

Eric Samuel Timm is a master. He takes the heart of the ancient spiritual masters and their understanding of spiritual disciplines and translates them into the modern world without losing anything in that transition. Deep spirituality is gained at a great price. The ancients knew this, and the modern world needs to know it as well. Eric accomplishes this marvelous task with artistry and depth and engages the reader while telling this timeless story.

—DR. GORDON ANDERSON
President, North Central University, Minneapolis, MN

Over twelve years of criss-crossing with Eric across the nation, I've learned there is no substitute for my time with Jesus. In *Static Jedi* my good friend Eric Samuel Timm invites you and me to reset, turn down the volume, and experience the supernatural. Jesus is calling—let's go.

—NICK HALL
Evangelist, Pulse Founder

I've known Eric for many years now and have toured with him all over the country! He has to be one of my favorite people to be around: one, because of his genuine love for God, and two, because of his hunger and thirst to see this generation changed. I can't wait to see the impact this book will have on many young people!

—LEELAND MOORING
Recording artist, Leeland

Static Jedi—humorous, heartfelt, and very helpful! Eric in his own unique style of writing will challenge and inspire you to step back and prioritize your relationship with God. I can tell you that he lives out the words written on these pages, and after reading this book, you'll be living them out too.

—MIKE LOVE
Executive director, YC and Extreme Dream Ministries

STATIC

JEDI™

STATIC JEDI™

ERIC SAMUEL TIMM

PASSIO

Most CHARISMA HOUSE BOOK GROUP products are available at special quantity discounts for bulk purchase for sales promotions, premiums, fund-raising, and educational needs. For details, write Charisma House Book Group, 600 Rinehart Road, Lake Mary, Florida 32746, or telephone (407) 333-0600.

STATIC JEDI by Eric Samuel Timm
Published by Passio
Charisma Media/Charisma House Book Group
600 Rinehart Road
Lake Mary, Florida 32746
www.charismahouse.com

Scripture quotations are from the Holy Bible, English Standard Version. Copyright © 2001 by Crossway Bibles, a division of Good News Publishers. Used by permission.

Cover design by Justin Evans
Design Director: Bill Johnson

Visit the author's website at www.nooneunderground.com.

Library of Congress Control Number: 2013942831
International Standard Book Number: 978-1-62136-271-5
E-book ISBN: 978-1-62136-272-2

While the author has made every effort to provide accurate telephone numbers and Internet addresses at the time of publication, neither the publisher nor the author assumes any responsibility for errors or for changes that occur after publication.

First edition

13 14 15 16 17 — 9 8 7 6 5 4 3 2 1
Printed in the United States of America

To all those who have given grace when I failed.

To those believing and acting upon what
Jesus wants to do through my hands.

To my entire family. Lose battles but win the war
for love together. I fight for you with arms laid
down. May your muskets forever lay as well.

To X and Z. May you always be strong new houses for the
King that defend mankind. I'm proud of you and who you
are yet to become. Awake. Love. Think, and then speak.

To my window, my compass, my anchor securing
deeply. Your reflective radiance confirms what
I always knew. The only real color is you.

CONTENTS

Foreword by Mark Batterson...........................xx

Preface..xxii

Acknowledgments.................................... xxvi

Introduction of a Perspective xxvii

Chapter 1: Are You a Static Jedi? 1

Chapter 2: Clocks and Cash 18

Chapter 3: Oil and Water 33

Chapter 4: Just Butter, Baby 47

Chapter 5: Twin Stones to Stand Upon................ 57

Chapter 6: Pseudo-Static Masters..................... 65

Chapter 7: Quasi-Static Masters..................... 79

Chapter 8: Noisy Lives = Noisy Churches = ?.......... 94

Chapter 9: The Static Master (Part 1):
  Jesus Rose Early and Withdrew 104

Chapter 10: The Static Master (Part 2):
  Jesus Memorized God's Word 116

Chapter 11: The Static Master (Part 3):
  Jesus Fasted and Discipled........................ 124

Chapter 12: New Beginning 137

Chapter 13: Green Men Speak Truth................. 146

Chapter 14: Early Arts of Drawing and Prayer 154

Chapter 15: Swords in Hotel Drawers 164

Chapter 16: Hungry Copy Machines.................. 182

Chapter 17: The End Is the Beginning................ 193

Epilogue 199

Notes 201

FOREWORD

WHAT IS NOISE?

Maybe a better question, what is "white light?"

If you have ever gone through a school lesson on what makes white light, you remember seeing a rainbow refracted through a piece of triangle-shaped glass from a single light source. White light is made up of all the colors, and each is seen when slowed down long enough for the frequencies of light to be displayed. This happens usually in form of the entire rainbow cascaded into a component of colors.

In the same way white noise is constructed of many frequencies. From the science of light is where we get the term *white noise*, because it shares similar properties. White noise is a combination of different frequencies. In fact, perfect white noise would be defined to the human as all the imaginable tones that a human ear can hear. It's why it works so well. Your brain can easily hear one person speaking but continue adding voices, and eventually we can't pick out anyone; it all becomes noise.

We are living in a time where the hearing from God is bombarded by many frequencies and voices. This noise, corrosive in nature, makes it difficult to hear God's voice...living with more noise means we live less like a disciple.

We need a prism.

Eric Samuel Timm is a prism.

A remarkable artful communicator of God's truth who personally is mastering the medium, he challenges you to see, hear, and then do. In the pages ahead Eric illuminates what has been there all along...to see the frequencies, hear from God, and live more like a disciple.

God is using him to help me see what was there but not so easily apparent until revealed in a moment.

This book you're holding is also prism.

This book cuts the noise.

This is your moment, to hear, see, and do.

Mary had a moment of revelation. Simple yet so profound. Imagine Mary after Jesus was crucified. All the thoughts raging inside her head and heart. The noise of the circumstance, of the Roman soldiers, the trial days earlier, and even the judge internally in her own heart. Then something cuts through it all. Her name is spoken by her Rabbi, Jesus. The light becomes color...the white noise becomes a singular voice.

What was true then can be true for you. Let the noise print of the world, circumstance, and settings fade. Hear His voice print over the sound compounding.

The rise of the kingdom of noise over your life doesn't have to conquer your life. There are many kingdoms but only one kingdom.

One little "k" Eric so timely addresses in the pages ahead is the kingdom of noise. So in closing collectively, as members of the same body, allow this book to help build the same kingdom to better serve the King. I encourage you to read it, walk your church through it, and share with the ones in your community to strengthen your community.

Be a master of the noise and live life in full color. In abundance, as Jesus so clearly states in John 10:10, "I have come to give you life full!"

See what you have never seen. Hear what you have been missing. Live how you have never lived.

—MARK BATTERSON
New York Times best-selling author, *The Circle Maker*

PREFACE

Noise.
It's everywhere.
Daily we are bathed in distractions. The noise
    intensifies, weaving strings
  around and through us
  until we are dancing under these powerful
    puppeteers.
These cords that can be broken, pull and tug, while we
    live a pseudo sense of control.
Daily surmounting, the noise is getting louder. We
    discover
  new noise,
  new sound.
Rather than protecting the ears of our hearts, we are
    drawn in each day like the fading
  tides that dance daily with the moon. The noise
    becomes a deep part of our everyday
  cycle, our now
  hurried lives.
Once immersed in the noise, we struggle to hear clearly.

In my travels, I am often asked,
"Who am I supposed to be?"
"What is God's will?"
"When do I know?"
"Where was God?"
"Why can't I hear God?"
"How can I ever move
  beyond my past,
  on,
  forward?"
In this noise we decide, direct, dictate, and die.

At one time, the noise did not so easily roam.
    Connected was a horse to a cart.

Clarity was vital to life.
In any generation there was—
    is—
    a deep need for clarity,
Not circumstantial to surroundings, cycles, events, or
       trends.
Continually bathed in noise, we begin to unravel.
Life is a dangerous place to stupor about when you are
       a slave to the noise, stripped of
    the ability to hear clearly. Your daily ritual baths
    have left you feeling anything but
    clean. In the mire of noise your questions are
    breeding and birthing more questions,
Which remain unanswered.
Such offspring are like fruit,
    spawned from the tree of noise,
    not born of the tree of life.
Often God speaks life in the stillness, apart from the
       noise. When Elijah needed to hear,
    God sent
    a strong wind,
    an earthquake,
    and a fire.
God wasn't in the wind, in the quake, or the fire.
He whispered in the stillness.
Noise hides this stillness,
    clouds direction,
    breeds pain,
    doubt,
    fear,
    confusion.
Our core cries out for God to answer, to speak.

Maybe God has already said what we wish Him to say.
    I wonder if it's frustrating for
    God to see us holding His Word while we ask for
      answers He already gave.
Are we asking for directions with the map in our
      hands?
With different characters but the same plot, sometimes
      our story has already unfolded.
    It's just trapped in the pages of ink and paper.
God is waiting
    in His Word.
Our hunger for His Word must outweigh the very
      thing that weighs us:
The noise.
Our life must contain clarity where we decide, direct,
      dictate,
    and live.
The noise must become a slave.
Once mastered, it is a useful tool.
To position your life differently, reverse your actions.
    This will change you.
Your life's cyclical tides will dance
    not with the moon
    but with the Son.
Do the natural. He does the super.
Embrace your freedom!
Live a life of clarity.
Become like the Master.
Master your noise.
Master the static.
Become a Static Jedi.

Static Jedi: One who masters the noise. Noise, existing in many shapes, consumes our time, real life, and ability to hear God. A Jedi is a form of master, teacher, and sensei.

ACKNOWLEDGMENTS

A BIBLICAL SAGE ONCE scribed, "There is nothing new under the sun."

In these same truthful words I would say this book is not my own.

It is not so much that I have written this book but transcribed this from the many people who have first inscribed these pages upon my heart.

Their effort validates their extensive writing as their cramping hand reminds them of who they are. I give back your text in form of this book.

For the writers upon my heart have been more than just scribes to me. So yes, there is nothing new under the sun.

However, through the Son, as a son, all things are new.

Within a desk drawer or unearthed from within the deep mines of myself are all new when illumined by a father or mother.

I acknowledge my fathers and mothers.

Thanks for being dads and moms.

The kind that have changed history, mine.

INTRODUCTION
OF A PERSPECTIVE

I CANNOT EXPLAIN THE arrival of the words I've penned in the pages that lie ahead in your field of view. Only by God's grace and the faith to strike the keyboard with the fingers He made upon my own hands has this book come about.

By grace through faith.
Grace from what Jesus provides.
Faith from my response in this provision.
This is the perspective.
The pages ahead can easily be read from a different
    view.
The words penned are not found rooted in what we
    have to do or are to earn.
Jesus has completed and paid what we cannot.
The journey to master the noise, becoming a Static Jedi,
    is not a *have* to, but a *get* to.
It's a choice you get to make, as it is so with love, faith,
    and hope.
The purpose of a motivational book is to get you going.
The end game of a self-help book is to get you to
    change.
The prize of an inspirational book is to get you to feel
    better.
The goal of this book is worship.
Journey to be found before God alone, reeking of
    worship, not of the noise,
as a master of it—
a Static Jedi.
So take a journey with me through these pages.

I only offer the same path I myself have walked.
    The path Jesus walked as well.
Not from a haughty assumption and my own spiritual
        trophy case, but a conviction found in God's Word
        and the way the Word lived.
    I can't guarantee that you finish the book, but I can
        safely say that if you do, you will feel as I felt when
        I completed it,
    Changed.
    Challenged.
    Equipped.

This path I speak of from noise to stillness,
    from passive to pursuit,
    knowing about to knowing Jesus is not only mine to
        personalize and travel.
That being said, I have offered a road post at the end of
    each chapter.
Questions.
Questions that you can ask yourself, internally (internal
    inquiry) or within a group setting, externally
    (external inquiry).
These will help guide you and make the pages I
    personalized to myself and my story come alive to
    then be personalized to you.
The person you can become will not recognize the
    person you are now.
Read on to not finish but to change.

Chapter 1

ARE YOU A STATIC JEDI?

EVERYONE MOVES AT some point in life. To an apartment, house, college, or hut. We are transient creatures.

I remember moving when I was a kid. A family relocation means a new place, new schools, and lots of unknowns. I was fine with those. What I didn't like about moving was the packing. I had to pack, haul, and then unpack. I didn't like having my room torn apart or having to reset everything as it was.

I have never met anyone who likes the ancient ritual of moving. When my cousin recently told me he was moving, he said it with that special "This is really going to stink" tone in his voice. Moving is work, and it's emotionally, physically, and financially draining. Going to a new address requires time and money, and once you've moved in, you have to hunt for the television remote and the pizza cutter. They are probably in the same box. After our last move the cutter was nowhere to be found, so I used my wife's scrapbook scissors with the zigzag edge to slice a frozen pizza. My favorite thin crust never had such beautiful lacy edges.

In our recent move things were lost, one after another, into the black hole of the moving space continuum. For weeks I couldn't find critical proprietary pieces for a shelf unit. The shelves wouldn't go together, and one of the missing pieces is probably only found on a remote island near Sweden, so I couldn't dash to the local hardware for replacement parts. But then, during the final walk through of our old house, like a retired beach bum I raked my son's backyard sandbox and found the missing piece. If you wonder where something is, check the sandbox. It's rule number 346 of parenting. Rule number 347 is buy a new pizza cutter.

On moving day I stacked boxes containing my earthly belongings into the truck. One box on top of another, I built a huge cardboard wall. Soon the belongings—the pizza cutter, the incomplete shelving unit, and my turbo nose trimmer—stacked behind the wall were no longer visible.

I think our lives can become a lot like that cardboard barrier.

Build a Wall

Think about your average week. Consider your daily routine, specifically how you invest your time. More specifically focus on your level of noise—those tasks you know don't really matter. The urgent and not-so-urgent that pull you from the important. This noise would be those things that distract us, not including work, school, sleep, or our daily commute. We'll look at the overarching installments of each day as we continue on, but for now let's focus on the noise.

How many hours do you invest every day ingesting your noise? Total the investment of your time in hours from all the different sources of noise in your life. What would your noise number be?

For me I've had to ask how many hours in a day, collectively, I'm on the Internet—clicking, checking, swiping, updating, posting. How much time do I invest watching television and movies, searching YouTube for a laugh, or playing video games? Where am I choosing to entrap myself in endless conversations scribed one text line at a time? How many hours, collectively, am I glued to a screen? With my phone in hand, bending my gaze toward my Facebook, Twitter, and Instagram accounts takes minutes at a time, but when the reality is compounded, it takes up much more, maybe even hours.

This could include non-digital forms of distraction too, such as newspapers, magazines, board games, and romance novels. (No, I'm usually not caught reading romance novels; however, you may be. Your noise currents may be different from mine. Different generations and different people have different noises, but all of it is still noise.) Make a note of the hours you invest in noise each day. Write this note in this book (if you are reading a hard copy), your journal, a napkin, or your digital notepad.

For this example let's say you honestly invest two hours each day immersed in your noise. Maybe it's way more for you. Maybe it's less. Whatever the case, be honest with your number and generous in your definition of noise. I say to be generous with your definition because sometimes we rationalize the noise until we're convinced what we're doing and hearing is actually building substance into our lives. I see this concept most prevalent in the current landscape of social media. We justify our actions and interactions with noise as educational or relationally productive.

Is it? How do you know? How can you be sure?

Now let's take that daily number in our example of two hours per day and multiply it by seven days in a week. Two hours each day in the noise x seven days a week = fourteen hours invested each week in the noise.

Let those fourteen hours be represented by fourteen cardboard boxes. Every hour in the noise is represented by one box.

If your daily noise number is one, then you would have seven boxes here. If your number of noise hours is three, you would have twenty-one boxes.

For our example now we're going to multiply fourteen boxes per week by the average number of four weeks in a month. This is simple mathematics. I'm not trying to do quantum physics, account for a leap year, or figure the gravitational pull of the earth during the winter solstice of the southeastern hemisphere. If you have your calculator app or old-school TI-85 calculator with you, put it away. There will be no graphs. Or you can draw one if it makes you feel better.

At just 2 hours per day invested in noise, our 14 hours each week multiplied by 4 weeks in an average month equals 56 hours per month. In a month we have built a wall consisting of fifty-six cardboard boxes. In a year that number grows to 730 hours, being that there are 365 days in a year. If you divide 730 by 24, it equals about 30 days—meaning that approximately 1 whole month out of each year of our life is invested in noise. What if that math is applied to 10 years of your life? The result from that application can be startling.

It's a slippery slope, and we slide it blindly. Sliding down further than we realize at just two hours a day invested in the noise.

In one decade we fall just shy of losing an entire year to the noise—at only two hours a day.

That's almost 10 percent of your life spent investing in the noise.

We are often unaware of the gradual decline and the erosion our lives but not unaware of the gnawing feeling it brings.

If you feel that gnawing, that pull within you to focus on what really matters, that call within to live differently, then you are becoming aware of this and are no longer blind to it.

Without awareness change is difficult.

If you don't adjust the math, then every ten years you live your life, you will have lost about one of them—to the noise.

A year of your life: that's watching the screen for one year. That's twelve months you failed to live.

You merely existed. Like a banana slug. Which are yellow and have one lung. Wild West yellow too—not a color you want to be labeled.

Breathing in, exhaling out.

A half-life.

Turn twenty years old at this rate of investment in the noise and that's two years of your life lost searching YouTube for treasure. The treasure chest was empty, a pointless quest the reward. At forty years old, the traditional midpoint celebration of life, about 10 percent or so of your life will be gone to the noise at just two hours a day invested in it.

Your child turns ten years old, but to you, he or she is still nine because you missed a year. Almost twelve months of not being face-to-face in relationship with your kids.

Instead, you were screen to face.

They were in the other room.

This may not apply directly to you if you're not a parent. However, if you are as I am, you may be haunted by the number of hours you spend together with your kids. The time you spend so easily decreases when you factor in hours of school, church, music lessons, and a couple summer camps. Children are only children for a brief number of years, and that goes by too fast. For some the rate of responsibility is even faster as kids are pushed into adulthood in our society of the fatherless. It doesn't have to be this way. The amount of noise in our life potentially steals an additional two years away from what has been said to be the cornerstone of culture and successful communities: the family.

But back to our wall, which is another rising cornerstone of culture, the noise.

Wall of Noise

In one month we have fifty-six cardboard boxes that each represent an hour of noise. To build our wall, let's put seven boxes in a row and stack another row of seven on top of those seven. Eventually we have a wall that is seven boxes wide and eight boxes tall. The wall of noise.

Walls keep things out.

Walls keep things in.

We hide stuff behind our walls.

Walls have gone up, come down, and remained strong throughout the history of the world—the Great Wall of China, the Berlin Wall, the walls of a city called Jericho, the walls of our hearts—to name a few.

The Bible tells us that huge walls surrounded Jericho. Some archeological evidence argues there were actually two walls and that Jericho stood on a hill. At the base of the hill would have been a stone retaining wall that rose twelve to fifteen feet high. Built upon that retaining wall was possibly a mud brick wall some six feet thick and twenty-six feet tall. At the top of this hill, where Jericho perched, was a second mud brick wall.[1]

Both sides of any historical/archeological debate can agree Jericho was an impressive structure for its time. Possibly towering fifty feet into the sky, the Jericho fortifications must have appeared intimidating as the Israelites marched around the walled structure—I know they would have for me if I had only a handmade spear in hand.

The story in the Bible ends with the walls coming down.

Do the Math

Let's begin to tear down our walls of noise.

Standing in front of our example of fifty-six boxes, we can remove them one at a time—but how we do this will be a special process. Just as we thought about our average week and how we invest time ingesting noise, let's do that again now, only from a different angle.

Instead of focusing on noise, now concentrate on the time you invest in clarity. This is time devoted to things that change us, grow us, and draw us to become more like Christ. Moments when the sands of the hourglass do not slip through our fingers, but when we instead grab hold of every precious grain. These are the occasions spent with Jesus and the moments that really matter.

It's this communing with clarity that moves us toward becoming a Static Jedi.

One who masters the noise.

If you placed a number on how many hours each day you

invest in clarity, what would that number be? How frequently do you remove yourself from the noise? How much time do you spend in meaningful conversation, breaking bread, engaging face-to-face with your family, or fasting in private? How many hours or minutes in a day, collectively, are you praying, seeking, reading, or memorizing the Word? How much time do you invest in bringing the balance back to where God's voice is the loudest or withdrawing to the stillness of the morning? Do you, even in the chaos of the day as you're stuck in traffic or baptized in the hustle of life, find ways to continue to focus on acknowledging the presence of God?

As you are at this moment, what would you say? How much time do you invest in clarity?

Clarity Defined

We live in a busy time. Always moving, perpetually in motion—tasks, distractions. We are so adequately named the human *race*. Always running. *Human race* is a spiritual classification and condition, far more than just a sociological label.

In an age where time just speeds by, we can easily, carelessly, and foolishly squander it. But here's the thing. No one can retrieve time already squandered. Each day our twenty-four-hour allotment is typically invested in rushing around with tasks, school, homework, cleaning, kids, sleep, and our jobs. I've had mornings when the first thing I do after waking up is grab my handheld digital noisemaker and check statuses and e-mail and then fight fires—putting out urgent and unimportant matters with my limited life's energy and my finite twenty-four-hour allotment. It's like a cosmic eight ball that I can't get out from behind, and then the cycle repeats. There are days when my breath seems like something I can never catch, and enough is never enough. Then I end days like this by turning on the fan or a digital noisemaker to sleep.

We need the noise to sleep, to rest.

The silence has a foreign nature to it.

It's too quiet.

It's uncomfortable.

It's out of place,

out of pace,

with our lives.

We've all felt this way, and if we're honest, these days turn into weeks, then months, then years. This habitual way of living creeps into the chambers of our hearts and diverts and dictates our life-giving flow. Unless we are purposeful and watchful regarding our daily moments, all those precious minutes are ruthlessly stolen by the noise.

Except on Sunday.

Sunday is always the Sabbath at home, right?

Nope.

Too often Sunday becomes the catch-up-and-prepare day—catch up the loose ends left over from the week before and prepare for the onslaught that's coming in the week ahead. It's nothing like a Sabbath day, remembered and set apart. So how much time would you put down in pursuit of God and clarity?

 Clarity is silently and stealthy exchanged for noise. #staticjedi @ericsamueltimm

Every time I ask this question when I'm speaking and painting at churches, conferences of young people, or with leaders in ministry, it gets really quiet. The silence and personal stories reflected from the audience tell me that sometimes the Bible is not even opened in a given week. Christ followers are more apt to rake over a quick devotional than shovel and dig into God's Word by wrestling, studying, and memorizing it. I'm not looking for spiritual trophy-case displays here, but it burdens my heart as I meet followers of Christ who can quote copious amounts of movie dialogue and music lyrics but can't give me five verses by heart from God's Word.

Even for a hundred bucks. (Some of you were there when I tried this at camp one time. I still have the hundred-dollar bill in my office!)

The Word and prayer dwindle to something dashed off perfunctorily before we eat or go to sleep—if then. Church becomes a social club or a box on the to-do list that we check off for the week. Discipling others gets lost in the shuffle of life, as we have left the path long ago of being disciples ourselves. The only thing we are caught withdrawing to is anything that keeps us from withdrawing from our toxic addiction to noise. For many, it isn't an illegal substance we fear withdrawal from. It's that spiritually toxic addiction to the static, to the noise. It's easy to stay hooked in our full world. We despise the morning and don't ever have to really feel hunger pangs.

Clarity is silently and stealthily exchanged for noise.

In fact, countless devotionals and study Bibles are based on the concept of getting our clarity in two minutes or less. This trains us to think there is "time with God" and "our time." The compartmentalization of His voice to set times we commune with Him is a dangerous place to live. Is it our goal to spend the slightest amount of time possible with the Lord and still be in relationship with Him? I'm not discounting the effectiveness of these publications or their place in our lives at certain times, but their very existence validates a system that tries to battle the noise with the least amount of commitment—just like a specific type of soda in your grocery store indicates a precise kind of beverage-drinker guzzling down that exact flavor of food coloring or aspartame. (What exactly is caramel color, anyway?)

Noise is battled fifteen, ten, and five minutes at a time.

But do you think it's working?

As the body of Christ, are we winning this struggle?

Has it worked for you?

Are you still a servant—or, more truthfully, slave—to the noise? I'll let you decide.

Continually packaging God's Word in compact and easy-to-use ways will continue to produce compact and easy-to-use followers of Christ—who possibly have compact dreams and easy visions.

Devotionals and Shaving

That's why I think some devotionals are like shavers. Manufacturers started out with one blade; then they added two blades. Later they determined we need two blades and a lotion strip. OK, wait—three blades, a gel strip, and an AAA battery with a heater and automatic lotion dispenser with a tanning application. Then a fourth blade for that really close shave, and by the way, it's got an MP3 player with a thumb drive in the base, and it runs on both operating systems. And it has to be pink.

Or red.

The overarching marketing message here is the need to make it faster and easier with the least amount of effort for the consumer.

Workout videos are the same way. Eight-minute abs, five-minute abs, two-minute abs, one-minute abs, and then buy the electric belt and it works it out for you with electrostimulation.

Like automatic sit-ups without the *up*.

Just the sit.

Just sit and enjoy your popcorn—the *up* is taken care of.

This easy, quick, convenient mentality has compartmentalized our walk with the Lord. The one-minute Bible and quick devotions are aimed at us. What are we teaching about time spent with God?

What's next—the thirty-second study Bible?

Maybe we should just make Christianity microwaveable. Something like Microwaveable Christianity Hot Pockets.

Or maybe God would like us to show up once in a while without it being fast and easy.

And calling the crowd to him with his disciples, he said to them, "If anyone would come after me, let him deny himself and take up his cross and follow me. For whoever would save his life will lose it, but whoever loses his life for my sake and the gospel's will save it."

—MARK 8:34–35

Maybe the life Jesus is talking about here is our social life—that rapidly expanding, partly cyber, private-yet-public social life.

But maybe He just means our life, which raises a few questions:

What is our life?

What makes up our life?

What is the life Jesus is talking about here?

The breath that enters our lungs?

The house we live in or the pursuit of the one we wish to own?

Our math class?

The political party we belong to?

Our opinions?

Our experiences?

I say all of it.

The word *life* in Mark 8:34–35 is the Greek word *psychē*.[2] It is a powerful, colorful word that means "breath" or "the vital forces which animates the body and shows itself in breathing." When we see the breath leave a body, it then stops the perpetual motion of breathing. We then understand this as life having left their lungs. *Psychē* also refers to "the seat of feelings, desires, affections...(our heart, soul, etc.)."

So the better question may be, what feelings, desires, or affections in our lives are seated where they shouldn't be?

The noise.

Since we are all body, soul, and spirit (1 Thess. 5:23), we all have the same basic moving parts to us. In Christ the spirit is made new and is connected to the Spirit of God. Our bodies are simply our shells, the package for the spirit and the soul.

But the soul is the battleground.

The noise is focused on eroding the soul.

We store much in the soul. The soul is where we remember. The soul is where we remind ourselves what was, not always what the Spirit of God says is.

Like a flash drive or hard disk in a computer, we record our lives, will, experiences, opinions, and emotions—all within our souls. Thoughts, feelings, personalities, and dreams...it's no wonder there is a struggle within us to get the soul to continue to align with the spirit. What the spirit wants must overcome what we want so the mind and then the body can follow.

It's a struggle for the throne of hearts, for the seat of our minds. The noise constantly wants that seat.

To be on that throne.

This sacred throne of our soul is what the enemy seeks to occupy. So maybe the life Jesus is saying we should be laying down is a life that involves anything that is seated where He should be.

This could be an exhaustive list of things such as our past or future, callings, dreams, money, kids, time, talents, Facebook, opinions, and anything or everything that encompasses us and the earthly kingdoms we build with our hands, from paycheck to paycheck.

This is the life, the *psychē*, we are to lose.

There are no shortcuts. When we lose our life for Him and for the gospel, we save it.

Maybe it's not that important to watch that movie. Maybe we'll pick up our cross for two hours instead. Possibly we should go serve the poor or make a tangible two-hour difference in someone's life through our own sweat and earthly effort to bring a heavenly result. What if we got up early, before the ones we love, to pray for the ones that need love? What if we hungered for God more than food?

Maybe we should start asking ourselves questions like that.

I started asking myself those questions, and God started

showing me answers. Of course, they were answers I *needed* to hear but not always ones I *wanted* to hear. You know what I mean?

It's not an easy road to become a Static Jedi.

It means a shedding of distracting noise.

It's also a shedding of darkness that wants to distract.

Maybe the darkness knows the noise too?

The devil's minions are captured speaking with each other in *The Screwtape Letters* by C. S. Lewis. This collection of fictional letters are addressed to Wormwood, a new tempter, from a senior devil, his uncle Screwtape. In letter #22, "How to Recognize Noise and to Resist Avoiding the Silence," we listen in on the perspective and goal of the Kingdom of Noise, as Lewis calls it:

> We will make the whole universe a noise in the end. We have already made great strides in this direction as regards the Earth. The melodies and silences of Heaven will be shouted down in the end. But I admit we are not yet loud enough, or anything like it. Research is in progress.[3]

Research yourself to make new progress on this path. It's a path littered by pieces of yourself as you walk closer to Jesus. Chunks of who you are fall down, and who you're becoming walks forward.

It's our first nature to be a slave to the noise, but your spirit man is crying out to be a slave to the King. If to live is Christ and to die is gain, we need to bring back the death of life.

But we don't like to die.

Death is scary.

Calculating Clarity

So, again, how much time would you write down?

How much time do you really invest battling the noise each day?

You will have to do your own math. But you have to answer honestly. I can't answer this question for you, but there is an answer.

Once you have your answer, take the number and multiply it by seven. That will give you the amount of time you invest in clarity each week, whether in hours or minutes.

If you answered in minutes, take that second number and divide it by 60 to get your weekly number of hours. For example, 30 minutes each day times 7 is 210 minutes per week, divided by 60 gives you 3½ hours spent in clarity each week.

Now multiply that number by 4, and that will give you close to the number of hours you invest each month becoming a Static Jedi—one who masters the noise. Some of us have 5, 14, or 26.3 hours of clarity invested in a 4-week period. You may have only 3 or 1 hour. Maybe you have just 20 minutes.

Whatever your number, know that your future awaits you. Be encouraged to know that God is revealing something new to you even now. When we feel as if our past actions overshadow our future, His Word assures us He is simply doing a new thing. For years you may have felt your faith was a wilderness. Or maybe recently you've found yourself more connected to the things of earth than the things above. But even in these wastelands God is making a way, and there will be fresh, life-giving water there. People God uses significantly often spend time in the desert, but they don't stay there.

The desert is a place we die.

It is also the place new life is birthed.

> Remember not the former things, nor consider the things of old. Behold, I am doing a new thing; now it springs forth, do you not perceive it? I will make a way in the wilderness and rivers in the desert.
>
> —ISAIAH 43:18–19

If you are willing to pay the price, the person you become won't recognize the person you are now, once you get to the point of becoming that new person. When you get there, you'll do more for your current world, helping others find who they are to become in Christ too.

If you read history you find the Christians who did the most for this present world were precisely those who thought most of the next.[4]

—C. S. Lewis

Think most of what matters.

Think less of what doesn't.

For change to occur, there will be a cost, and there is a price.

It's paid when no one is looking.

Without much private discipline in the mastery of noise, there is little public reward in piercing it. We need to follow Jesus back to how we should best live with clarity.

Let's get back to the sword. Let's be people of the blade, God's Word. Through His Word we fall in love with Him more, and because of this we love more.

Can you feel it? Change is in the forecast—a 100 percent chance of the Son shining upon you. Walk into the light, out from the noise found in the shadows.

Change takes place when stress is placed upon the target, and it begins with something stirring in your heart. For this internal shift to continue, you must begin to master the noise by journeying to become a Static Jedi—a form of disciple and sensei that masters the noise that exists in many shapes and consumes your time, your real life, and your ability to hear God.

So let's begin—today.

For you, greater things await.

Today, Begin

The first step toward those greater things is tearing down your walls of noise and purposefully investing your God-given time into what truly matters, exchanging clarity for every box of noise you eliminate.

For every hour you invest each month in clarity, you get to take down one box from your wall of noise. So stand in front of our example of those fifty-six boxes of noise, and let's start removing them. Start bulldozing your wall from the top, one at a time.

How far did you get?

A Static Jedi lives to have no walls. Now, if God didn't like walls at all, we would have nowhere to hang awesome Christian bookstore art. But the walls God doesn't like are those that stand between us and Him or that stand in front of where He wants us to go.

Just ask Jericho.

■ INTERNAL INQUIRY ■

1. How tall is your wall?

2. What has been the source of noise in your life?

3. What could be sources of clarity in your life?

4. How do you define clarity or time with God?

5. Movie lines and song lyrics or the Word of God—which means more to you?

6. Does our level of knowledge reflect our affections?

■ EXTERNAL EXCHANGE ■

1. How much of our lives have we failed to live?

2. What are the walls of noise in your life keeping in? Keeping out?

3. Are we "over-noised"?

4. What did you feel God spoke most to you through this chapter?

5. How can we pray for each other as we ask God to help us dismantle our walls?

6. How many hours are you surrounded by your noise each day?

Chapter 2

CLOCKS AND CASH

TIME IS MONEY, so...let's go!"

The phrase reverberated around the dirty grease kitchen ravaged from the day's breakfast rush. Food scraps had formed an "everything" omelet on top of the stainless steel work area. The words echoed off the hanging pans stained with flame and then danced through the cooking smoke until they reached their intended target: my sweaty ear canal.

There I stood, on summer work from Bible school, called into early action from the ranks of a simple buffet table server to whip up fluffy omelets in the kitchen, in place of the main breakfast cook who had decided to drink more than his little liver could handle. Thanks to the years of mom-chef boot camp, though, I was prepared to answer my call into early culinary duty.

Determined to learn on the fly, I took on the challenge, working as fast as I could because, after all, *time is money*.

We've all heard that phrase—countless times, no doubt.

If not, just give it time.

"Time is money."

There. You heard it.

But is it, really? Are time and money equivalent?

Time is a form of currency—this is true. However, currency, or money, is something we can get more of. Of course, money is not found on a shelf at the store. Most of us don't have a money tree we can visit to pluck paper and metal fruit from its branches. But we can get more. Legally or illegally at the bank, there is money waiting for us.

The most common way to acquire additional green is by trading time for dollars. We are compensated with renewable currency for punching the clock, doing chores to cash in on our allowance, or carrying out our salaried duties. Because our time has value, time is a form of wealth.

However, unlike money, we simply cannot commandeer more time. Once time is gone, it has flown forever. There is no endless supply. Time is the currency before which all other currencies bow.

When we are bankrupt in the richness of time, the outflow of our lives becomes hurried and undervalued. Time may feel different on occasion, but it's the same amount mathematically. Occasionally time feels slow, and with each wretched click of the clock we watch it drag.

And drag.

Ask any student stuck in the self-induced prison of detention, watching the second hand click through thick, dark molasses.

 Time is the currency before which all other currencies bow. #staticjedi @ericsamueltimm

Then there's the way time felt slow—like life moving in slow motion—when I kissed my wife for the first time.

Summertime flies by, though, and we wonder where it went. Holiday breaks, our wedding day, the first three months of a new baby's life, our children's childhood, our forties.

If we look at time the way the ancient Mayans did, believing that time exists because our events do, then we may find a way to defeat time. Remove the events and time disappears.

Right?

The truth is we will always have events, large and small, so we will always have time. Like gravity on earth, we cannot defeat time, only master it.

Everyone on the planet has the same allotment of minutes each day. No more and no less. There are 24 hours in each day, 168 hours in a week, and 8,736 hours in a year, and each one ticks by one millisecond, second, and minute at a time. Like sand though the hourglass, our moments slip away. Sometimes we capture the sand, and other times it falls quickly between our fingers. A day is too precious a treasure to forfeit.

But we convince ourselves there will be tomorrow. Waiting for the next day is like the slogan at my favorite place for pie in Harmony, Minnesota. The servers wear shirts that say "Free pie…tomorrow." Come back tomorrow and read the same shirt.

I've decided to buy the pie today. Don't wait for tomorrow. Rally to the cry of Mr. Keating in the film *Dead Poets Society*: "Carpe diem! Seize the day, boys. Make your lives extraordinary."[1]

Too many people never catch tomorrow as they let go of today. They fail to capture the precious now and miss out on what they hope tomorrow will hold too.

You and I are given a daily life allowance of twenty-four hours. Time is the currency of life—like money.

The Greenbacks of Our Lives

Money has a magical appeal. It's a power force and an even more powerful puppet master. Once mastered, it can be a life flow for the giver and receiver. In Numbers 11, after Israel escaped slavery in Egypt, the rabble voiced its greedy desires:

> Now the rabble that was among them had a strong craving. And the people of Israel also wept again and said, "Oh that we had meat to eat! We remember the fish we ate in Egypt that cost nothing, the cucumbers, the melons, the leeks, the onions, and the garlic. But now our strength is dried up, and there is nothing at all but this manna to look at."
>
> —Numbers 11:4–6

We may not be in the wilderness like they were, but the rabble is still heard on every channel, in newsprint, and online through pay-per-click ads. Keeping up with the Joneses is our modern-day equivalent of tuning in to the rabble of Numbers 11.

Earthly treasure—money—is made of paper and metal. Paper has unlimited uses. We can use it for writing, for building Wright Brothers paper airplane replicas, and for wiping. Toilet paper is made of the same raw stuff as the stuff in your wallet, pocket, purse, or 401(k). This will keenly shape your perspective and help in emergency bathroom situations where paper is sparse.

Metal too makes up lots of things—arches, ape hangers, aircraft wing assemblies, anchors for ships. Boat anchors can be a burden to carry onshore outside of their intended purpose, or they can be an indispensable asset to a ship's crew set adrift.

So it is with money—it can be a burden or an asset.

Jesus talked a lot about money. In Luke 16:10 He says, "One who is faithful in a very little is also faithful in much, and one who is dishonest in a very little is also dishonest in much."

It doesn't matter if you have a lot or a little money. It's what you do with it that determines its power.

Is money a tool or an idol to you?

It depends on the posture of your heart toward it. We can spend money on gum, movie tickets, food, and gas for our SUV or hybrid car. (I drive a Prius. In a related story I turned in my "man" card, but they gave me a "green" one to replace it.)

Our currency easily escapes our grasp, spent daily on little things and occasional big things. Buying on credit, we trade our callings, dreams, and freedom for a nicer car with not-so-easy monthly payments.

One of my first decisions with my wife was to buy our first car. I wanted this 2003 GTI Golf twentieth anniversary edition in Imola race yellow—just one of two hundred fifty made with 1.8T, a side-mount intercooler, Recaro racing buckets, cold-air intake, a Dieselgeek short-shift kit, Porsche-vented breaks, a K04 upgrade, front and rear sway bars, an upgraded central ECU, Bilstein coilovers, NEUSPEED cat-back, a down pipe, a GReddy turbo timer, dual exhaust, all rolling on 18-inch BBS 2 part wheels. Basically a legal race car.

My wife wanted the Volkswagen Beetle, with the flower vase built into the dash. Basically a rolling prom bouquet.

Like all good marriages that last fifty-plus years, we came to a compromise. An agreement. A middle ground, so to speak.

We got the Beetle.

If you didn't laugh, just wait a few years after you're married. You'll see a pattern emerge. (Love you, honey.)

But do we spend?

Or do we invest?

Investing in Honey 101

Investing is a simple concept. No black suit or subscription to the *Wall Street Journal* is needed for you to get this next part.

Let me break it down for you. Instead of buying honey, you want to own part of the honey farm that will give you a portion of the profits from others trading their money for that honey. This payback is called dividends.

Another way is to grow the part of the business you own. This is simply the farm's stock price. Buy low; sell high. You buy part of the honey farm when it is just a mom-and-pop operation, and then the farm goes factory, gets huge, and mom and pop no longer bottle the honey—they just have their picture on the label and a large home in Spain. When this happens, the part of the farm you own increases in value.

We invest money into savings accounts, stock market plays— otherwise known as intelligent gambling (cough, cough)—a 401(k), bonds, land, real estate, and our kids' college savings plan. Looking at dividends, payout on interest rates, and company-projected values, we seek a high rate of return on the money we've invested, or ROI. A higher rate of return means more value. More value means mo' money, and mo' money means… (If you said "mo' problems," you are thirty years or older and liked rap music.)

A high rate of return ensures a place to stockpile the blessing and abundance we have been given. My small amount saved for the future is not so small compared to the amount my brothers and sisters in Christ make rummaging for recyclables in the Nicaragua trash dump to make $400 yearly.

But my bank savings statement reminds me I have never seen a hearse with a trailer hitch pulling a U-haul packed with money and possessions. We don't dig two holes for the dead—one for them and one for their stuff. Remember this.

We trade money for gum, or honey, or honey-flavored gum, and we occasionally invest in retirement, school, and stocks in the hope of receiving good dividends. We never spend money. We only invest it. Everything pays a return. That gum you buy pays a dividend in the form of fresh breath. (Others enjoy that investment.)

The honey pays a return, as it's pleasurable in tea and on toast.

Spending money on a gaming system, a boat, a new shirt, or a DVD pays a brief form of return in entertainment before decreasing in value as those things sit and become outdated on the shelf or in the driveway.

Everything we spend money on pays a form of return.

Even if the return is zero.

While "zero" has no multiplying power, don't underestimate its value. Math is not possible without zero casting its thick, valueless shadow.

Valuelessness is possibly the most powerful value.

Here's what I mean. Sometimes the payback is outweighed by the cost. Our investments can rot, decay, be stolen, or be multiplied. Greater things are seen—maybe not directly by us—when we give to Jesus what He entrusted to our care. Give Jesus what you have, and what you give will never lose value; it will only gain. If you keep what you should give to Jesus, then your eye has seen what you kept in its largest form of value.

Our investments in earthly things can rot, decay, be stolen, or be separated from us.

However, if we give Jesus what we have, what we give Him will never be less.

Greater rewards are seen—maybe not directly by us—when we invest into Jesus. It will always pay higher return.

By keeping, we keep things small.

By giving, we expand them.

I used *we* because it's Jesus and us working together with whom He is and what we have despite what we are not.

A boy, faith, a willing heart, a simple lunch, and Jesus paid a high dividend.

Jesus multiplies our investments—just like fish and bread.

But we never spend money on fish or bread, remember. We invest in them. If we partake in eating, the nutrition to our bodies is the return on our investment. If we share them with others, the joy in giving them is our return.

We never spend money. We only invest it. Everything pays a return.

Everything.

Time, Traded

Just like money, we never spend the currency of our lives. Time is not spent. Not gambled. Not traded. Not even given.

Time is invested.

Sometimes the return is immeasurable, and sometimes it's a loss. Invest time in homework, and your return is knowledge and good grades. Invest time in your children, and the payout comes later in life in the form of their confidence, honesty, and integrity. Time invested in your children yields memories. Time invested in your marriage pays back each year for hopefully fifty-plus years.

Invest time in exercise, and the dividend may be a healthier heart and a keen mind. Invest time in *Guitar Hero,* and you may have mastered a plastic guitar, but the payout will be pretty low. Grab a real guitar and try the same Santana riff for a totally different story. Invest time comparing yourself to everyone else, and this comparing spirit returns nothing but negativity to you. Invest time focusing on your past, and even though it has been separated as far as the east is from the west, you seat what has already come and gone in a place of present power.

Crazy Grandma Lorraine

Each summer my Grandmother Timm visited us for a week. She showed up with crazy big hair and piano necklaces to drive us around in her huge baby blue Buick.

Life with Grandmother Timm was good. Real good.

When shopping with our mother, stacks of multicolored sugar cereal loomed out of reach. Like two puppies hopeful for a treat, my sister and I would stare at the Trix bunny and salivate. We saw Lucky Charms, Count Chocula, and Cap'n Crunch. We mustered enough courage to ask, to present our request before the queen, and our mom would kindly say the statement no kid wants to hear in the cereal aisle: "No."

Then she'd load the cart with regular Cheerios and kid-tested, mother-approved Kix.

But when Grandma brought us to the grocery store, it was open season on sugar. We had our license from the Department of Natural Resources, and sugar is a natural resource. We were ready to hunt us some sugar! When we got to the cereal aisle, where the hunting is real good, Grandma let us pick any kind we wanted. Two boxes! Each! Sugar Puffs, Apple Jacks, Corn Pops. The only way to decide was to scan for what treasure, decoder, or mail-in toy certificate lay within. (I never waited for the box to be empty to retrieve the toy. Just dug to the bottom, coating the cereal with my skin cells for everyone to enjoy. Hungry?)

When we arrived home, Grandma would make us sit on the

couch while she hid the cereal. It was a true sugar expedition to find each box. A lot of effort for cereal.

Looking back, it was never about the cereal. More than clicks on a clock, my grandmother's investment of time in my sister and me shaped us and gave us much—including cavities.

When we invest our life's currency into things that matter, mastery is possible.

In valueless time mastery is also possible—the mastery of nothing.

Read that again. It's good. Jesus told me to write it.

Mastery \\'mast(ə)rē\\ n 2 a : possession or display of great skill or technique b : skill or knowledge that makes one master of a subject.[2]

Throughout history, heroes had one thing in common: they were masters of their craft. We are never remembered for what we are good at; we are remembered for what we master.

One hour at a time.

Your Investments

How do you invest your time? Let's find out.

Get a wallet, envelope, billfold, coin purse, or that plastic coin holder businesses used to use as promotional items that I always thought looked like plastic lips. (Why would my bank want to give my mom and dad plastic lips?)

To do the following exercise, you may have to go to your bank and use your lips. Ask the teller to break down twenty-four dollars, denarius, or yen—or use Monopoly money and coins. Get twenty-two single dollar bills, and then make two dollars out of quarters, nickels, dimes, and pennies. The mix of coins is not important as long as the combination of twenty-two one-dollar bills and coins equals twenty-four dollars.

Now put the money in your envelope or wallet or hold it in your hand.

These twenty-four dollars represent the twenty-four hours in every single day. Let's invest our daily allotment using the money to represent our time and see where it goes.

First, count out sleep. I love sleep. I dream about it. Without rest we become cranky or even sick. All creatures need a form of rest. If you have little kids, you get less sleep. If you're a youth pastor or volunteer and do those all-night lock-ins—which are renamed at 3:47 a.m. to be called "hell on earth"—you are not getting paid enough and really throw the math off for this illustration.

During our normal routine, humans sleep. So count out seven dollars in bills to represent seven hours of sleep, and set them aside.

Twenty-four minus seven dollars subtracted for sleep leaves us with seventeen dollars.

Work or school is typically an eight-hour daily investment. If you're salaried or taking night classes, it may be more or it may be less. Count out eight dollars in bill form and set them aside.

You now have nine dollars remaining in the original stack of twenty-four dollars we started with.

Next, we invest time throughout the day to travel—walking to and from class or our next appointment, driving kids to school and lessons, driving to and from work, and so on. According to a Gallup survey, people average 45.6 minutes commuting to and from work in a typical day. Let's round it to an hour each day burned up in hall crossings, windshield time, or on a pedal bike keeping all things green.[3]

After deducting a dollar for travel, eight hours of your life's daily currency remains.

What about personal hygiene? Are you that older sister in the bathroom who spends two hours getting ready? Or do you never shower? Either way, that's a problem for the others in your life.

Do you prefer to find a nice quiet, private, clean bathroom where you can grab a magazine or play your Nintendo 3DS? My grandfather threw the math way off on this one. When he went into the bathroom, it was, well, an event. He would go in and come out the following week with the Encyclopedia Britannica A through L in hand, read all the way through. I wondered if there was a secret door in his bathroom that he used to sneak out. I could only hope he would escape to a magical workshop for hours to make toys for the children of the world. What I'm saying is Santa possibly makes toys on his toilet time. That is multitasking. Reading on the toilet is possibly the only time men multitask.

OK, remove one more dollar from the stack for extended personal time, showering, bathing, and other getting-ready routines. Our twenty-four hours, or bills, are now down to seven. Five single bills and two dollars in change should remain.

Now we need to carve out time to eat. I love to eat. I love to make food, then serve food, then eat it and end with dessert. But meals have become rushed, hurried, and distracted. The typical mealtime is far closer to bearing its secondary fruit of nourishment to our bodies than its original intention of providing a time of fellowship and rest.

Most of the workforce and student population has a half-hour for lunch. Figuring a conservative hour prep-time, execution, and clean up of each meal in a given day, count out a dollar bill.

Four single bills and two dollars are left. Six hours remain.

Now grab the remote, and let's invest some television time. As a kid my favorite show was *Saved by the Bell*. I wanted to be A. C. Slater, but I looked more like Zach Morris.

The average person watches several hours of TV daily. At my house there are days the TV is never on. Other days I watch a comedy with my wife, a marathon on a network, or a movie with my kids.

For the consumption of pleasurable or informational programming via TV, movies, DVDs, and possibly newspaper reading, deduct one dollar to represent one hour a day.

Three single bills and two dollars in change should be left in your "time" pile.

Now, how many hours a day are you on your smartphone or in front of a computer on a social network? Maybe you endlessly search sales, products, blogs, and YouTube. What about composing personal e-mails? For the 4.8 billion people on Twitter and Facebook, social media has become an integral part of the day. I know it's a part of mine. (I'm on Twitter at twitter.com/ericsamueltimm and Facebook at facebook.com/ericsamueltimm.)

In this private and public arena we send information about ourselves to the worldwide interwebs and have "friends" we don't really know. For many it has crossed the threshold of something we control to something that controls us. This constant connectedness keeps us connected to those not in the room while keeping us disconnected from the ones who are.

These digital forms of communication and information gathering can quickly supersede the remaining currency of time we have left. If that's the case, you're overspent and in debt to what could be a source of noise in your life.

For a conservative two hours on the Internet, pay out two dollars.

Now, three hours of our original twenty-four remain, represented by a one-dollar bill and two dollars in change.

Talking on the phone and text-messaging happen throughout the day. Talking to and texting parents, friends, kids, and the pizza delivery guy easily add up to a half hour. Depending on your age, other things such as sports, homework, working out, laundry, banking, yard work, or basic housework can consume an additional hour each day.

Count out $1.50 from your remaining stack.

Only $1.50—or ninety minutes—remain.

Coins in hand, raise your arm over the countertop.

Let the change go.

That's a familiar sound of change clanging. Maybe it's the exact sound God hears each day when we bring Him our leftovers, giving Him what we can scrounge up in the couch cushions of our lives—and expecting a high rate of return on the investment, no less.

God may not like change, unless it's our heart.

Giving Jesus no time, or a specific "devo" time slot, breeds guilt or piousness that comes with the check-box life. So why bring Him your change or further set aside part of your day as "devo time" and expect a high return on your investment?

If we are cheap with our relationships on this earth, we can see firsthand the effects of our stinginess. If we continue to be conservative in our pursuit of God, our love for Him will remain conservative. But can we easily overlook our stinginess?

There have been times I've said with white knuckles, "I'm going to do long daily devotionals every day!"—only to get off track about mid-January, after all those resolutions become history and we become extremely discouraged with our lack of solid follow-through.

A bookend experience hanging out on the other end of the shelf is when, after spending that scheduled time with God, I've responded to my family or a situation in a way so very unlike Christ amid the sea of noise.

Maybe you can relate?

It's important to concentrate part of each day for personal fellowship with the Father through prayer and the study of His Word, but that can easily be the only moment we speak with Him. Is there a rich and rewarding alternative? A way to take on Christ's yoke that's internally restful?

Yes. Become a Static Jedi.

Become a student of the Master, again, or for the first time.

A scholarly quest it is partly, a spiritual one fully.

The word *scholarship* from the Latin word *scola*.

Translated from this root form meaning "free time."

This quest is investing differently but also about protecting the time you have to call "free."

This spiritually scholarly time comes only at a cost to the less profitable investments.

It is impossible without expanding the margin.

The blank space in your life.

Masterless mastery is obtained when battling without creating space.

Battling this noise is creating space for God and acknowledging the space He occupies,

which is all of it.

Invite God into *all twenty-four hours* of your day.

Seek God through devoted investment,

but also through determined involvement.

This is the path of a Static Jedi. Jesus becomes part of the currency. Intentionally not investing time with Jesus or intentionally excluding Him from the rest of our time does not make us into masters of the static.

Rather, it compartmentalizes our walk with Him.

Jesus loves to walk with us.

He loves to be with us all the time—

not just in the scheduled

time or in the leftovers.

The only change He wants is our hearts.

Let's change

by rearranging the change.

■ INTERNAL INQUIRY ■

1. Where have you invested the currency of your life with a low payout?

2. Is your life overspent?

3. Where are you investing your time overall? What's the ROI?

4. Is money your tool or your idol? How does this affect the investment of your time?

5. Are you giving God your "spare change"? What needs to change?

■ EXTERNAL EXCHANGE ■

1. What's the first thing you invested your money in this morning? What was the ROI?

2. How can we invite Jesus into our twenty-four hours rather than giving Him the leftover change?

3. What do you think our most valuable resource is? Why?

4. What excuses do we make to wait for tomorrow for something good God wants us to do today?

Chapter 3

OIL AND WATER

Pour oil and water together, and they refuse to mix. A chemical tension and resistance exists on a molecular level that keeps the two from playing nice. They separate, and very apparent is the clear divide between the two. This occurs on a catastrophic level when an oil tanker or sub-oceanic pipeline splits open. Once the money pipes are dumping liters of crude oil into the ocean, you'll see the black cream rise to the top.

Water mixes with other liquids to form solutions—especially with two cups of sugar, red #40, and flavoring on a hot summer day. Kool-Aid is the taste of childhood summers. (I like to double the sugar in the recipe on the side of the box and consequently double the kidney stones.)

As for the oil and water relationship, science explains that the density of the two are different. The poet would say it's as if they're from two different worlds—the Capulets and the Montagues.

Like oil or water, we approach mastering noise from two different sides of the tracks. Two different ways of looking at the world.

Christian or non-Christian.

Which one are you?

Beyond hobbies, employment, family relationships, and convictions, we can boil it all down and see there is one of two worlds we come from. Oil or water. We may currently be living in a Christian home, surrounded by Christian influences, or living in a non-Christian home, surrounded by non-Christian influences.

Christian or non-Christian worldviews.

Oil or water.

Past or present.

Whatever your past or current surroundings may hold, the noise can be mastered. If you are surrounded by faith in Jesus or surrounded by faith in other things, people, or gods, this mastery of the noise is still yours to grasp, and yours alone.

One perspective does not have it easier than the other.

I hope that someday things are not so divided into neat subcultures. This us versus them mentality has to be replaced and supplanted with grace. I hope for a time when rock bands can make music about their Creator and we don't have to decide what "market" they operate in. Oil or water markets. A time when the word *Christian* ceases to be an adjective but remains what it is supposed to be: a noun. This is when Jesus comes to town.

Everyone needs Jesus in their town.

However, He won't arrive, because He is already there.

We just all need to look more like Jesus.

We all need more of Jesus.

This is your personal responsibility. It's possible to seek more, but this is an everyday, every moment decision. Just like faith.

> And without faith it is impossible to please him, for whoever would draw near to God must believe that he exists and that he rewards those who seek him.
>
> —HEBREWS 11:6

God loves a hearty faith stew. This full-flavor faith stew consists of two main ingredients:

1. An overflowing measure of reception

2. An abundant quantity of rejection

Reception that our lives need no other ingredient than Jesus Christ.

Rejection of the belief that we are enough.

This reception and rejection is possible for those who had either Christian or non-Christian upbringings and surroundings. The decision toward faith is equally accessible to both. Faith, and the finding of faith, may be influenced by environment, but the decision remains our own.

Jesus died for Jew *and* Gentile, for oil *and* water. He seeks that which was lost and sets free those bound up in religion. History was forever changed when God so loved the world that He gave His only Son. Now we are each invited to know Him. To have a relationship with Him. Without believing and confessing God's gift of forgiveness and reconciliation through His Son, Jesus Christ, we are separated from God. Because of faith in Christ and His grace, we are reconciled to the Father. "All this is from God, who through Christ reconciled us to himself and gave us the ministry of reconciliation" (2 Cor. 5:18).

Just as you could first decide to follow Jesus no matter your surroundings or history, it's also possible to discover who we are through Him rather than who the noise pulls us to be. The noise of our past and our surroundings can try to hinder us from mastering the noise. It labors to keep us from putting on our new identity in Christ. Further, we can hinder our own selves.

The rub is that we easily identify with who we used to be, before we were in Christ. It's as easy to slide back to our familiar habits as it is to settle into a worn dip in a mattress. Our nature, surroundings, and past wrap like strings around us, and soon we are focused on the unimportant, lacking conviction and dancing to the flat notes of the noise, only to speak occasionally with a shallow tone and weak voice.

We go back to what we know best: the noise of our old self.

Is there something better for us?

Stolen Identity

Sometimes followers of Christ claim their old identity.

I'll give you one example.

"I'm just a sinner saved by grace."

A sinner. Hmm.

> Therefore, if anyone is in Christ, he is a new creation. The
> old has passed away; behold, the new has come.
>
> —2 Corinthians 5:17

I have to tie myself to the anchor of who He is and who I am through Him. The Word says I was a sinner saved by grace, but through Jesus, the old is gone and the new has come. You and I sin, but our identity is not a sinner. See the "but" in that last sentence? Buts are great, but not everyone realizes they have them. In God's Word there are big buts, little buts, and butts in the form of donkeys. The Bible is filled with "buts" and a whole collection of "used to bes." Put them together, and it's a powerful equation.

Used to be a tax collector, but…

Used to be a leper, but…

Used to be a corpse, but…

In Christ you are a "used to be." You *used to be* a sinner. But in Christ we are no longer sinners. We sin, but that is not our identity.

Change the song.

 The Bible is filled with "buts" and a whole collection of "used to bes." Put them together, and it's a powerful equation. #staticjedi @ericsamueltimm

This identity crisis most easily haunts those who are slaves to noise. The noise pulls us back to the old melody of who we used to be and hides who we are in Jesus. Through Christ we have a new identity, so we should not be speaking to our old man, the sinner, and giving him his identity back. The more we act on our pursuit of Christ, the more we discover who we are.

Discover the treasure of who you are in your new identity through Jesus by mastering the noise that seeks to place you on a treasureless path.

Know Him, not *of* Him.

Know who you are through Him and less of who you are without Him.

> Therefore, as you received Christ Jesus the Lord, so walk in him, rooted and built up in him and established in the faith, just as you were taught, abounding in thanksgiving. See to it that no one takes you captive by philosophy and empty deceit, according to human tradition, according to the elemental spirits of the world, and not according to Christ.
> —COLOSSIANS 2:6–8

Actions Speak Louder Than Words

You speak to your old self with your actions, not just words. Actions can speak louder than words, in fact. When we don't take action, we foster the mistaken reality of our old identity. Salvation isn't the issue at hand here. The goal isn't just to "get in."

I've lived in the dangerous place of living like I know Christ, when in reality I knew a lot of noise and a lot about noise, but I only knew *of* Jesus. And by grace I never want to return. I don't want to live a religious check-box life, nor do I want leave the Father's side.

Let's think about this in terms of a story Jesus tells that's found in the Gospel of Luke. It's a story of two sons and their father. Naturally the father loves them. In the story he is found on two separate occasions waiting upon each of his sons to draw near to him. One son stays near the father and lives his perfect check-box life. The other son goes away and squanders his wealth, life, and everything the father had given him.

Few are they who by faith touch Him; multitudes are they who throng about Him.[1]

—St. Augustine of Hippo

The father is caught in the story waiting and waiting and waiting for the boy that left his side to finally come home—until one day his wait is over. With nowhere left to turn, his wayward son decides to return home. Upon the return of his boy, the father runs to him, accepts him, and throws a huge party.

This is viewed by the other son—the son who never left—to be an undeserved celebration, and it's more than he can stand. After all, there was no celebration for him and his right living that he'd done along. In his mind he's the deserving one, not his dissident brother. So in protest he refuses to join the celebration.

The father leaves the party, escapes to the other side of the door, and begs this beloved son who has been there by his side all along to come in and celebrate the return of his lost brother. After pleading with his son, in a failed attempt to convince him, the father escapes back to the party on the other side of the door. There the father is left waiting, waiting, and waiting, for his son does not enter when the celebration rings for his brother's arrival home.

The story ends at that moment, but it continues today. And while many revelations exist within this story, I care to focus on the father.

God is the father, waiting on the sons.

He is waiting on you.

But the noise has had your attention.

In the story it was possible for either son to take action toward the father—to either come into the party or just come on home.

The same is true for you.
Take action.
The father will respond.
Abba is waiting.

Oreos and the Rapture

There is no question about whether a dad loves his child once the dad has assembled a bike. Bikes used to come in a box, and it was a process just to get the two-wheeler road worthy. My dad put together my Huffy bike one Christmas after I opened the gift by ripping the paper and box to shreds.

I still remember that first ride at Easter.

(Assembly was a little harder than expected.)

Riding home from school on that Huffy bike was the highlight of my day. With that last class under my belt, I had a new sense of purpose: riding to Chuck Little's store for blue moon ice cream. Pedaling with no hands, I arrived home with an ice cream in each hand.

One time when I got home, both my parents were gone—and like any normal pastor's kid, I instantly thought the Rapture happened.

I was left behind.

I had sinned that day, so it was over. The *Thief in the Night* video I had seen at Royal Rangers would be my new reality.

In my panic I searched the church directory for the phone number of a board member named Mr. Elward Engle. When Mr. Engle prayed, not a missionary on the world map in the church foyer was left unmentioned. When we played basketball, he wouldn't even get mad—I would be furious at a bad call, and Elward would be cool as a cucumber.

On this pre-tribulation occasion my parents were nowhere to be found, so I dialed up Mr. Engle. The conversation was pretty short.

"Hello, this is Elward." He had an earthy, James Earl Jones voice.

Pause.

"Hello, this is Elward," the one-way dialogue continued.

Click.

As soon as he picked up, I knew the Rapture hadn't happened. If anyone was ready to see Jesus, it was Elward. He wasn't going to miss it. This I knew.

But more often than those post-apocalyptic scares, my mom was home to welcome my sister and me. A quick after-school snack, consisting of a sleeve of Oreos and a half-gallon of milk, and it was outside to play football with the Moon boys. In between I would go say hi to my dad and buy a forty-cent Pepsi from the pop machine.

Dad was, and still is, a pastor. He'd be doing his normal daily routine at church, and after finishing my after-school sugar buffet, I would walk through the side door of the parsonage and up the back part of Thompson Hall. Usually Dad wasn't in the office behind a desk. Nor was he downstairs setting up chairs. As I got closer to the sanctuary, I could hear the worship music. Once I heard the music, I knew where he was: on the front row, near the organ that Delbert Greenman played, Bible open on his knees. My father was in prayer. That image is ingrained in my heart, along with the orange 1978-style carpeting on the floor of the church.

You could incorrectly assume this type of Christian experience while growing up would facilitate an easy transition for me to find and pursue God. I grew up in a Christian environment, and my greatest worldly influence—my dad—is a God-chaser. As a child of God, Dad daily pursued the person of God, mastering the noise and living in the realm of clarity.

Yet even in these secure insulators, I had to make the decision to know God rather than know *about* Him through secondhand faith. I had to deal with my wall by investing my time differently. I had to journey to become a Static Jedi.

If I had made that decision earlier in life, years would have been invested, not just spent. So much time slipped through my hands that I cannot get back.

Those hands would have directed the symphony of my life differently if I'd come to know God sooner. I would never have used that hotel pen to write my own suicide note. The pen would have stayed next to the hotel pad where it had been placed, used to write a pizza order for a family or to collect the numbers for the hotel Wi-Fi passcode.

For some people the greatest testimony of faith is the prevention of pain. Others experience radical redemption from a path that threatened to consume their life. We can be rescued from oil or water—and both are great stories. However, like grass being greener on the other side, oil appears darker or the water clearer. Our stories are as unique as our backgrounds.

My wife, Danielle, has a testimony that astounds. Like mine, a small part of her story involved coming home from school as a kid. However, she wasn't a pastor's kid. She didn't go to a church after school. Her journey home looked a little different from mine. Maybe yours did too.

Storms in the Garage

Danielle rode her bike over dirt roads, or sometimes took the bus, to the far corner lot with cows just beyond the electric fence— the same electric fence that I discovered years later while using the outside restroom behind the evergreens. (It was a *shocking* Christmas.)

A sister to eight siblings and now an aunt to the drove of nieces and nephews, Danielle is no stranger to the term *dull moment*. Through many seasons, both turbulent and peaceful, her family always remained strong together.

At home for one of these seasons, Danielle weathered a storm. For many years it rained at her house. Mostly in the garage.

Raining regret.

Raining an unsettled peace.

Raining fear.

All this rain drove like an inner storm in her father's heart. Dealing with the rain of pain is a challenge for each of us. Being around this type of rain gnaws a soul. Turn on the news and you see it raining all over the world, and it's tough to stomach. It's downright hard, but the answer is always the same: When you're in the rain, you need a covering.

A shelter.

An umbrella.

During the Old Testament Passover, the blood of a lamb covered God's chosen people. In the New Testament Jesus is that Lamb. In the Old Testament the blood was applied to the doorposts of a house. In the New Testament the blood is applied to the doorposts of our hearts.

Jesus Christ is our covering, and death has to pass over.

It rains on everyone.

It may be storming, but there is a covering. Life may be challenging, but there is a covering.

It may seem impossible,
hopeless,
doubtful,
fear-ridden,
and pain-laden,
but there is a covering.

> You have heard that it was said, "You shall love your neighbor and hate your enemy." But I say to you, Love your enemies and pray for those who persecute you, so that you may be sons of your Father who is in heaven. For he makes his sun rise on the evil and on the good, and sends rain on the just and on the unjust.
>
> —MATTHEW 5:43–45

We cannot control the rain, but we can control where it does not fall. In Danielle's life it rained around her. For a season the rain of fear and frustration made a daily appearance in the garage of her house. Danielle's father, I believe, simply forgot to turn to his umbrella. So the rain poured, and his shelter was different.

There are other umbrellas, but only one is red with the blood of Jesus.

Danielle's father sought shelter in alcohol. It's not uncommon. Boxes of empty beer cans stacked up in the garage. Occasionally the inner turmoil spilled over onto others. Verbal stones of silence hit hard. My wife and her brothers and sisters got bruised.

Despite the negative circumstances, my wife had a choice. She chose to pursue God and master the static.

She had to decide.

Years later my father-in-law, whom I deeply love, is a tender-hearted Irish man. Rough on the exterior but soft in his core, he is undeniably rich, with loving sons and daughters and thirty-something grandchildren. God is transforming his life! My goal is to beat him fairly at a game of croquet. (There is "good at croquet," and then there is "really good at croquet," and a few notches above that is my father-in-law.)

Whether you have a Christian or non-Christian background, it's possible to master the noise. Whether you're surrounded by either, it's your choice to have faith. Walking in your new identity in Christ is an everyday, every moment decision. The Father is waiting for us to take action.

We need to love Jesus more than the noise.

Here is the crazy part: the decision to love you has already been made. Before you do anything or become anything, God has already made the choice to love you. You were loved and chosen first.

Here's something even more insane: God already knows everything about you. Before you were born, before you were formed, He knew what you would like on your pizza, your favorite color, and your list of excuses.

> Before I formed you in the womb I knew you, and before
> you were born I consecrated you; I appointed you a prophet
> to the nations.
>
> —JEREMIAH 1:5

God already knows and loves you down to the molecular level.

Now you get to know and love Him down to your molecular level too.

Move out from under the thumb of the noise and know and love God like He already knows and loves you. Position your life differently so you begin to love differently. This is unfailingly possible for Christians and non-Christians, no matter their past or current surroundings.

Jesus is more powerful than your upbringing.

Jesus is more powerful than your journey, then or now.

Jesus is more powerful than the body connected to the hand that slaps your face.

Jesus is more powerful than the burns of someone's splattering, hateful tongue ripping across your soul.

Jesus is more powerful than your ministry.

Jesus is more powerful than your church's brand.

Jesus is more powerful than your lost or forgotten ability to trust and love a father.

Jesus is more powerful than your pastor dad.

Jesus is more powerful than the death that's loomed in your life.

Jesus has all the power inside and outside church. He is over our current surroundings and our past. He combines them and makes something new.

A New Dawn

The simplest way to combine oil and water is to add dishwashing liquid. Detergent, at the molecular level, is mutually attracted to water and oil, thus forming an emulsion. This chemistry is displayed in the natural when you wash those dirty dishes in the kitchen sink after you had company.

Displayed in the supernatural, detergent takes on oil or water through Jesus's love for all of us. He can have lordship over your past, present, and future noise. He is ready for you to know more of Him, not just about Him. Decide for the soundtrack of your life to be found in the hymnal song "Washed in the Blood." For this is a new dawn—just like the dishwashing soap.

> What therefore God has joined together, let not man separate.
> —MARK 10:9

Have you been to Jesus for the cleansing pow'r?
Are you washed in the blood of the Lamb?
Are you fully trusting in His grace this hour?
Are you washed in the blood of the Lamb?

Are you washed in the blood,
In the soul-cleansing blood of the Lamb?
Are your garments spotless? Are they white as snow?
Are you washed in the blood of the Lamb?

Are you walking daily by the Savior's side?
Are you washed in the blood of the Lamb?
Do you rest each moment in the Crucified?
Are you washed in the blood of the Lamb?

When the Bridegroom cometh will your robes be white?
Are you washed in the blood of the Lamb?
Will your soul be ready for the mansions bright,
And be washed in the blood of the Lamb?

Lay aside the garments that are stained with sin,
And be washed in the blood of the Lamb;
There's a fountain flowing for the soul unclean,
Oh, be washed in the blood of the Lamb![2]
—ELISHA A. HOFFMAN

■ INTERNAL INQUIRY ■

1. What has your journey home been like?

2. Do you believe change is possible for you?

3. In what ways have you been living in your old identity?

4. What stains in your life need to be washed?

■ EXTERNAL EXCHANGE ■

1. Are you from Christian or non-Christian surroundings?

2. How has this been a source of noise in your life?

3. What is your "used to be" and "but"? (I used to be
   _____, but . . .)

4. Why do you find it difficult to believe God loves you—and loved you before you were born, even knowing what you were going to do?

5. How should the truth of God's love help us live differently?

Chapter 4

JUST BUTTER, BABY

MORNING TOAST. ONE of my favorite meals of the day. The endless butters, jams, and spread choices create food art combinations that are mathematically astounding. According to Trader Joe's label, apple butter must have double the amount of fruit than sugar to be called "butter." It's a law. Anything less is plain old jam. File that in the section called "Who cares; it's delicious" or under random laws and street signs.

Salted sweet cream butter on a nearly burnt piece of Ezekiel bread is some good toast. "Mmm, good toast," to quote Nacho Libre. (Don't worry if you don't know who Nacho is; if you know, you know.) The butter sings as it melts and fills the little canyons on the sprouted grain surface. Are you hungry? Enough reading. Let's have a toast break.

Get some toast. Serious. Drive if you have to, or borrow bread from your neighbor next door. For my wheatless wonders of the world, get a gluten-free option.

Get some butter—salted butter, if you can. Or if you're not a friend of Mr. Lactose, use something like Mrs. Margarine instead. Nothing is better than real butter in my book. And this *is* my book. However, you bought the book, or it was given to you, so in that sense it's *your* book. But technically I wrote it, so it's mine. OK, it's your actual book, so we can compromise and call it *our* book, metaphysically speaking. However, this is my toast I'm making, and I'm going to use a sea of salted butter.

Once you have your bread, you'd better get your toast on. Toast that bread to your liking. I personally like waiting until I see smoke, just shy of flames, coming out of the toaster when I'm toasting my bread.

Once the toast is done, put that butter goodness on it—and in a special way. Not the way it's normally done, with a smooth swipe evenly distributed. Instead, clump a teaspoon in the middle of the bread and resist the urge to spread it out.

Let it soak.

Let it get melty.

After twenty seconds the tiny iceberg of butter dissipates into the toast.

Now, beginning with the crust, slowly eat all around the edge. It's pretty dry out there in no-butter land. The rich butter is in the middle, and we haven't reached it yet. But continue inward by munching around the center until only the center of the toast remains—about the size of a United States fifty-cent piece or a Canadian "two-ney."

In the center, by now, is a deep, fragrant pool of rich butter floating on the surface of perfectly toasted bread.

Eat that final morsel. That flavor-soaked middle. Delicious.

Where the butter was thin, the taste was pleasant. But where the butter was clumped, you taste the best and most flavorful bite of the toast.

The only way to improve on this bliss is to complement that last bite of butter toast with coffee. Now, good coffee is a relative term. You coffee snobs and connoisseurs know exactly what I'm talking about.

My pastor, Andrew Cass, roasts his own beans and occasionally shares a bag with me. His coffee brew is a smooth, dark, handsome Scorpio with that specialty Euro-roast goodness that I like. He gives me a little bag of beans—*little* being the key word.

He uses the smallest bag he can buy that Ziploc makes. Really, he must say to himself in the small plastic bag section, "What's the smallest bag I can get so that when I give Eric coffee, the bag looks full but it's only, like, one cup worth?"

When Andy gives me the coffee at church, it feels like an espresso drug deal going down. He passes me one of those little bags that's too small to fit a half sandwich, and I slyly take it into my possession. And with each exchange I want to pause and say a prayer for Andy's heart. *May his generosity increase because I crave his roasted coffee.*

The Other Mug

My morning coffee and toast structure begins early. I get up before the chaos wakes—two young sons, specifically, who are great at the beautiful distractions. Their words echo over the couch: "Dad, will you play cars with me?" In that instant my day is reprioritized. Learning to fulfill our children's requests is an art form vastly crippled when we're slaves to the noise—or immensely increased when we master it.

Each of us begins our day differently. We get ready for school or work or prepare for the day off. My goal every other day, even when traveling, is to beat everyone up in the morning—not with a right hook, but simply rising from my slumber before their day begins in order to get the good coffee and my toast on.

Once coffee is brewed, I pour a cup and place it in front of my seat on the table. Then I pour another mug and place it across the table from me, where it sits and waits.

My wife is still sleeping but soon will rise like the Kraken, consuming all the morning work and dirty laundry in the path to get to her cup of morning coffee.

But the other mug of coffee I poured is not for my wife.

I pour the second mug for Jesus.

He never drinks it—which leads me to believe He doesn't like the way I make coffee. Maybe I should try a French press or Pastor Andy's brew instead.

Jesus may not like coffee, but I think He likes having it with me. And maybe you should have coffee with Jesus too. How amazing would it be if all across the social media sites each morning we saw thousands of photos of people having coffee with Jesus. Communing with Christ over coffee. Instagram pics of lonely mugs look perplexing to one not familiar with this concept, but to God it is art.

Full mugs and expectant hearts.

Waiting on God.

Acknowledging His presence.

Listening.

Giving Him our day, each day, all day.

(It's a dream to see your pictures @ericsamueltimm on Instagram. I would suggest Lo-Fi filter.)

God invites us to start our day with Him and continue each day with Him every day. I have found it wise to accept His request. And I hope some morning I glance over at the mug I poured for Jesus and find it empty, supernaturally enjoyed by Jesus while I buttered my second slice of toast.

An Undying Passion

In the stillness I find my heart growing hot while I seek the person I have already found. God is so much more than I know. And He can be known as a close friend or lover. You can know God far beyond salvation.

If you want to.

Seeking God beyond the first encounter to find His personality, character, Word, desires, and will is necessary if we are to master the noise. Take the relationship past a casual encounter. Move along the pendulum toward an undying passion. This stokes the flames of your love for Him. It turns interest into passion, like into love, logic into illogical acts of faith.

Unlike finding something and no longer needing to search for it, we must continue to seek God beyond the initial finding. Jesus is perpetual discovery. Individually we believe and confess Christ, and individually we pursue the deeper treasure of relationship. From this personal pursuit a deeper revelation comes and a stronger personal relationship grows.

The starting point for the body of Christ corporately seeking God together is usually found where each leaves off in their personal quest. It's a powerful and mysterious relationship.

 Jesus is perpetual discovery.
#staticjedi @ericsamueltimm

We all bring something to offer—called gifts—to strengthen God's movement of love on this earth. If we want to know our God-given gifts, we must know the giver. God, the giver of these gifts, is moving in our lives, churches, schools, businesses, and families. Personal revival is us responding to Him. Historical revival starts with one strong personal relationship and is fed by many strong personal relationships. It's like a fire with many logs—the more logs, the hotter the blaze.

Want to throw more wood on the fire?

You must have strong arms to carry more wood.

So let's start growing.

Grow Some Grass

Ever had that neighbor with the perfect lawn? I do. Fred's lawn is an evenly cut, evenly green, four-inch-tall grass masterpiece. Look fast, and you would guess that it's more like AstroTurf than real lawn. Like a park, lush and green, his lawn remains perfectly cut without a single dandelion. I catch myself wishing I could play football with cleats on his yard. Or be like a snowboarder carving a path in fresh powder. Or take a snow-machine in Alaska where no snow-machine has gone before. Perfect lawns scream for a round of full-contact croquet. Or a mixed-martial-arts-mini-golf-lawn-dart match. Perhaps the gentleman's version of golf, with rakes for the massive litter boxes frequented by neighborhood cats.

Beautiful, lush, green golf-course turf is the best. I can't believe it's real grass at times when I'm walking on the fringe at a course. Guys with college degrees spend their careers perfecting such perfect grass. (No, not weed. I'm speaking of actual lawns.)

The grass is always greener on the other side—or at least we think it is. However, it never is; it's green where we water it. So let's get out the hose and attend to our own lawns of faith, shall we?

For many, what should be plush lawns of faith are instead sickly, dried-up, brown, dead, patches of grass. Lack of water results in a plague called *lack of personal pursuit*. This sickness is a product of a minuscule bacterium with massive complications called *complacency*. Self-satisfaction with our relationship with God distorts, slows, boxes in, or kills our pursuit of Him.

Dying lawns are sickly with a self-love that old-school hipsters and early philosophers knew as *amour-propre*. This is a condition that results in feeling OK with our current lawn of faith, even though it's dry and sickly. We settle, and so the noise easily settles in our hearts too.

This is because our love is easily selfish. The noise has to do with the version of love that we know. God's love is selfless, but self-love haunted mankind in the Garden of Eden. Adam and Eve communed with God, and He was not found in their little homemade boxes—until they chased the fruit rather than the gardener. They were convinced they needed fruit and not the vine.

Just one bite.

One self-satisfying morsel.

The philosopher François de La Rochefoucauld, who shaped pillars of French thought, explores the enigma of *amour-propre* by saying, "Self-Love is the Love of a man's own Self, and of every thing else, for his own Sake. It makes People Idolaters to themselves, and Tyrants to all the World besides."[1]

While we may not rise to the level of being a tyrant toward others, we easily become tyrants to ourselves, bankrupt save for a single introductory encounter with God—an encounter left to erode for lack of tending. In God's selfless love we see love gain its true power because a selfless love costs everything: "For God so loved the world, that he gave his only Son, that whoever believes in him should not perish but have eternal life" (John 3:16). God loved, so He gave. We never realize the power of real love unless we witness or experience a transaction, because real love costs.

Ahava Jesus

A word used for *love* in the Old Testament, *ahava*, consists of four basic Hebrew letters. Viewed through the modifier or lens of the Word, it translates to "I love" or "I give." To love is to give, and to give is to love. Down to the very way the word is constructed, loving and giving intersect.

What do you give to the ones you love? Time, money, life, honesty? The list goes on, because love costs. And real love costs everything:

> By this we know love, that he laid down his life for us, and
> we ought to lay down our lives for the brothers.
> —1 JOHN 3:16

Sometimes we need to start paying the price of a selfless love through the currency of our time—the currency of the hours we log on this earth.

The price paid for a relationship to grow with Jesus is the investment of our lives, and there will be a cost. Our relationship with Him must go beyond the first encounter. It cost us more than when we started. So we must love Jesus—*ahava* Jesus—more.

Coming to Jesus is the first step, but becoming like Jesus

is another process altogether and requires a selfless love. Discipleship means becoming like Jesus, not just filling our heads with knowledge, and it is not something we can do without dying to ourselves. It comes with a cost, and it's made with a choice.

Intense love does not measure, it just gives.[2]

—**Mother Teresa**

We must relentlessly pursue the revelation of who Christ is.

When compared to Christ, the things we hold tight are garbage. The endless media, social and antisocial engagements, things we find inside and outside of church, and the new, ever-changing, bright and shiny lures keep us from running toward the treasure that is Jesus. Throughout our lives we treasure this junk unless we consider knowing Him the treasure and those things the trash.

As you know Jesus more, you naturally love Him more. The less you know of Him, the less you love. To know Jesus is to love him.

> Indeed, I count everything as loss because of the surpassing worth of knowing Christ Jesus my Lord. For his sake I have suffered the loss of all things and count them as rubbish, in order that I may gain Christ.
>
> —PHILIPPIANS 3:8

Knowing Jesus is it. Once you begin to love Jesus more, everything in comparison, as Paul says in Philippians 3:8, is considered garbage.

Trash.

Not the treasure.

The refuse.

The leftovers.

Jim Elliot says, "He is no fool who gives what he cannot keep to gain that which he cannot lose."[3] To gain the treasure, you must leave the trash. The cost is all garbage anyway. It is a dangerous trap to believe our search is over because we gained all the riches we are going to have. The mysteries and abundance of God never end, but our time is limited. Only so many mornings in one life.

The cups of coffee we can consume are boarded in by time and space—the very thing God holds in His hand. This calculable, limited time on earth has numbered our days, and each of them must count. It is very difficult to hold the treasure of knowing Jesus and *amour-propre* in each hand, for one of the arms shall be lost. Which one will it be? That's up to you.

Tomorrow, rise before the rest of your world. While the coffee brews, make perfect toast crowned with a pat of butter. Have coffee with Jesus, and continue to lay the foundation in this quest to master the noise.

■ INTERNAL INQUIRY ■

1. How has your pursuit of Jesus stopped?

2. In what ways are you more concerned with what you can get from Jesus than just investing time with Him?

3. Could you have "coffee with Jesus" this week? What would that look like for you?

■ EXTERNAL EXCHANGE ■

1. What happens when we don't allow our lives to become rich in the pursuit of Jesus?

2. Have you ever heard Jesus speak to you in a still moment?

3. When did your faith became something that was real to you—or has it?

4. What parts of your faith journey need to be watered?

Chapter 5

TWIN STONES TO STAND UPON

WHEN IT COMES to pursuing God deeper, we need to remember two things. These are what I call the "twin stones" that we must stand upon in order to build a life that masters the noise. With these twin foundations, we become much like the pat of butter in the middle of that toast: rich with flavor.

Let's take a look at these two essential stones.

STONE #1: God Is a Person

God is a person, and you and I must pursue that person. Do we grasp this truth about the Father? We easily forget it. The static masters of the past, however, did not. The static masters of today won't either. Your heart must never forget that God is a person.

A person on earth, made in God's image, can be sought. People can live with each other for a lifetime and still be learning about each other. So it is with the Lord. Made in God's image, we desire to be known—just as God does.

 God is a person, and you and I must pursue that person. #staticjedi @ericsamueltimm

Do not strive to become a master of the noise for your vain remembrance. Heroes of the faith like Tozer, St. Augustine, St.

57

Francis of Assisi, and many others can and will inspire us, but we must purse the vine, the person of God, as they did.

> I am the vine; you are the branches. Whoever abides in me and I in him, he it is that bears much fruit, for apart from me you can do nothing.
>
> —JOHN 15:5

Jesus says it's not our job to produce the fruit but to pursue the vine—the person of God—which allows the fruit to grow.

My morning coffee break is about pursuing the vine, not the fruit. It's about pursuing the person of God, sitting there in front of me until the coffee goes cold.

This simple pleasure of having coffee with Jesus has radically changed my outlook on communing with Him. I have fallen in love with Him more. In this "more" I see less of what I need not see. My vision becomes fixed on love—or, in another word, Christ. I sit there, and the coffee sits there, and within that moment there lies the point. I wait a while, speak with Him a bit, and if Jesus doesn't drink His coffee, then maybe I have a second cup. Usually iced. And in this slow process of the degrees dropping in that coffee mug, I put skin on the standing stone that is the person of God.

A Static Jedi stands on this stone daily.

This is why the sacrament of Communion is such a visual reminder that Jesus, fully God and fully man, broke bread and passed the cup. He demonstrated how to remember what He was about to do on our behalf on a cruel cross, because He knows we easily forget.

> And he took bread, and when he had given thanks, he broke it and gave it to them, saying, "This is my body, which is given for you. Do this in remembrance of me."
>
> —LUKE 22:19

Pursuing the person of God is foundational to the mastering of the noise—to becoming a Static Jedi.

God is a deity that longs to commune with His creation. This triune God mysteriously exists in unity between Father, Son, and Holy Spirit, and He bridges every obstacle to be in unity with us—His beloved bride.

> The one who has the bride is the bridegroom. The friend of the bridegroom, who stands and hears him, rejoices greatly at the bridegroom's voice. Therefore this joy of mine is now complete.
>
> —John 3:29

Do you remember that God is a person, inviting you to know Him personally? As the bride of Christ, we need to seek out our groom. Like an earthly marriage, the groom continually seeks his bride even before the wedding day arrives. What happens if the bride does not seek the groom in return? The marriage does not have a different ending; rather, it just never begins.

You and I are in little…what God is in large.[1]

—A. W. Tozer

Eternal life in heaven promises joy and the absence of sorrow, but heaven is primarily about the coming together that happens after a pursuit that began on earth. It is the post-pursuit life.

Heaven will happen someday, but let's not wait.

Heaven can start now.

Pursue the King today and bring heaven to earth for yourself and others.

Place yourself in the eternal worship and pursuit of God now.

Beyond today, tomorrow, and the days that follow, the pursuit of God is not an isolated, one-time occurrence. This event does not start and end. It is not a task to check off on the spiritual to-do list. It's something that continually becomes.

The fullness of God cannot be known in:

- A leadership conference

- A couples retreat

- A youth convention

- A camp experience

We don't get to know each other in a single encounter—that first encounter is merely the beginning. So too we can't expect our heavenly relationship with the Father to be grasped in an initial meeting. Having spent nine months developing inside your mother's womb, you didn't fully know her after you were born. Nor can you know everything about your spouse the moment you marry him or her. Yet we easily lug around the expectation that we will know God fully once we are introduced to Him.

The idea is shortsighted.

If I expected this of my wife, our relationship would be shallow, weak, sickly, and anemic. After years of marriage it's only through the process of seeking her, pursing a friendship with her that's rooted in selfless love, and walking through trials both self-induced and circumstantial with her that I have even begun to plumb the depths of the woman who is my wife. Like the changing surface of a lively, pristine stream, she is fluid. Flourishing. Deepening. I will continually make new discoveries about my wife throughout our life together on earth.

Multiply that dynamic by infinity, and you'll start to come within a galaxy's proximity of the unlimited facets of God that can be known. And yet God beckons us to draw close and know Him.

What happens when we don't get to know God? The same thing that happens in relationships that don't include some measure of continual pursuit. For my relationship with my wife, Danielle, to thrive, I need to incorporate diligence and discipline in my pursuit of her. If we expect earthly relationships to be secure after one encounter, that's a recipe for marriages to fall apart and close friendships to become just casual acquaintances. When we fail to truly know others, we live on relationship islands.

Islands are sometimes remote. Hard to find. When we stop personally pursuing the person of God, we arrive on an island.

Alone.

The remote becomes local—and that's not as it should be.

The first step toward that isolated island is forgetting God is a person.

What happens in the natural happens in the supernatural.

Have you vacationed on that relational island apart from God?

In our passive pursuit of Him, self-assured that our finite knowledge of the Creator is sufficient, we relegate God to an island address without us, and then we go and live on a different island apart from Him.

And maybe visit Him on His island.

Once in a while.

When we need something.

Or when something bad happens.

Or when something goes well.

During the times I've felt separated from God, the first step toward my self-induced isolated island destination was always the same. He didn't go anywhere.

I did.

We do.

You did.

The route to this island, where noise reigns as the tyrannical dictator, is forgetting that God is a person.

STONE #2: God Has No Grandchildren

Most of us have families. We have mothers, fathers, brothers, sisters, stepparents, and cousins. We have grandparents. Known or unknown. Alive or deceased.

Born of a mother, all of us are the grandchildren of someone. As grandchildren we have grandparents who are elderly, beautiful people with "Pinterest-able" old furniture and, if you are lucky, pink hair.

Grandparents have grandchildren when their own kids have kids.

But God doesn't.

God is not a grandparent.

He will never be a member of the grandparent club. Ever.

He is a father, and He only has sons and daughters.

Masters of the noise live as sons and daughters of the King. Slaves of the noise live as grandchildren.

This second truth has shaped each revivalist, God chaser, and disciple of Christ, and not one of them, authentic in their faith, has lived as a grandchild of the King. It is a timeless principle that masters of the static will always live as sons and daughters. Never grandchildren. A secondhand faith, piggybacked on another who has a relationship with God, becomes a "have to," not a "get to" when it comes to the pursuit of God.

Your parents' faith will not carry you. Your grandparents' faith will not carry you. Your friends' faith will not carry you. Your parents' lack of faith will not carry you either. You do not inherit a "foundness" or "lostness" from your grandparents' spirituality or lack of spirituality. We must all come, as creatures created by God, to a place where we make the pursuit of God our own—not because we have to, but because we want to. The personal choice God gives us to make Jesus a part of our life is the starting point for each of us. In this place, identifying as a son or daughter of the King, we set another stone in the foundation to master the noise.

The twin stones that stand in clarity for us when we master the noise is remembering that God is a person and that He has no grandchildren. This foundation will foster your lawn of faith to grow and become deep and well watered. These two stones laid in the foundation of your heart will help keep you from being spread so thin you remain a clump of butter. Stand firm on this foundation.

How will you remember?

Choose to stand here or your feet will find other things to stand upon. You can easily build a life upon other stones, but that path leads to a false or partial life in the mastery of the noise. You become just a pseudo-Static Jedi or a quasi-Static Jedi. A false master.

■ INTERNAL INQUIRY ■

1. Since God is a person, how should that change the way and when you talk to Him?

2. Are you living on someone else's faith or your own?

3. How is Jesus found, beyond our first discovery of Him?

4. Do you have trouble seeing God in a personal way—as a person?

■ EXTERNAL EXCHANGE ■

1. What are the two stones to stand upon?

2. What can we do to remind us that God is a person?

3. What about the person of God do we need to seek?

4. What does it mean to you that God does not have grandchildren?

5. Do you see yourself as a child of God, or have you lived as a grandchild of God?

Chapter 6

PSEUDO-STATIC MASTERS

I TRAVEL A LOT. At times my life is summed up as a series of airplane delays and constant opposition to getting to where I need to be. Bringing my family is always a treat and usually saves me from purchasing small monster trucks to bring home for my sons. (For the record, Grave Digger is and forever will be the best. Also, I want to drive that thing. It's on my bucket list. Wait for it...and now it's on yours.)

Usually I speak and paint during a run of public school assemblies, a normal Sunday morning church service, or at a festival on a flatbed-trailer-turned-stage, up to the axle in a field of mud. All these events have one thing in common: people.

I'm continuously around people, sharing in their lives for a brief moment on the road or in extended moments at home with family and our community. Where there are people, there is food, and where there is food, there are people. (And bears. Unless you wrap everything in plastic and Eagle Scout your camping site.)

People tend to love food.

I know I'm tending—and usually tending a lot. On the road one of my usual highlights is eating at local food joints that require a three-day treadmill run to burn off.

It's great.

It's painful.

I truly enjoy eating excellent new food while having meaningful conversations.

But occasionally this spiritual act of breaking bread can get somewhat out of hand for me. Here's exhibit A. In the Colorado mountains, at an event called NYR, we decided to track my caloric intake for the day. I traveled from campsite to campsite, sampling meals and late-night delectables, including but not limited to homemade doughnuts over a fire, Dutch-oven pies of every kind, twice-fried s'mores, and something called a caramel heart attack.

Using the food-tracker application on his phone, a pastor friend calculated the calories. At the end of the day, I had (conservatively) consumed 11,235 calories.

Whoops.

That might be a week's worth of calories for a normal diet—and I had consumed them all in one day.

After seeing the total, I took three aspirin and went into the woods, where I found leaves and sticks to eat. I needed some heavy fiber, and I wasn't going to eat the cinnamon potpourri on the back of the toilet. That would be gross. I'm not a fan of cinnamon. It can make your mouth dry. If it was peach maple nut sunrise potpourri, I would have dove in.

Referencing an old *Saturday Night Live* skit, my pastor friend suggested a bowl of colon blow to aid the current crisis.

We laughed.

It hurt.

Logos of Logos

During these conversations over meals in many different settings and with many different people, I frequently hear book recommendations.

"Have you read this? You really need to check out this book."

Nothing is wrong with these recommendations, except it is

alarming to my core that I can count on one hand the times someone has said:

"Look at this amazing revelation from the Word."

"Eric, I have to show you this awesome story from Scripture."

"This passage has been speaking to me. Let me share it with you."

My publisher might not want me to say so, but this is a problem.

A pitfall for this generation is that we read more books with a publisher's logo on the spine than we do the Logos itself. Christians read more *about* the Bible than we do the pure Word itself.

At least I know I have. At times books about the Book have been all I've read.

 A pitfall for this generation is that we read more books with a publisher's logo on the spine than we do the Logos itself.
#staticjedi @ericsamueltimm

We can easily ingest more of man's words than God's. This produces a pseudo-Static Jedi in us though. A false mastery. We can find ourselves looking up from the bottom of this pitfall, needing to be reminded that Jesus is the Word. He is the very embodiment of God's Word.

Jesus has been sent to us—
the living Word.
The Logos has been sent to us—
the written Word.
Jesus is this Word.
The spirit of God bears witness to this:

> This is he who came by water and blood—Jesus Christ;
> not by the water only but by the water and the blood. And
> the Spirit is the one who testifies, because the Spirit is the

> truth.... If we receive the testimony of men, the testimony
> of God is greater, for this is the testimony of God that he
> has borne concerning his Son.
>
> —1 John 5:6–9

If Jesus was the Word and the Word became flesh, then shouldn't we know the Word while we have flesh? The more we know Him, the more we love Him, as we've already discovered. The less we know Him, the more Jesus becomes a mere interest.

> In the beginning was the Word, and the Word was with
> God, and the Word was God. He was in the beginning
> with God. All things were made through him, and without
> him was not any thing made that was made.
>
> —John 1:1–3

Interested followers of Jesus are uninterested in others. Lovers of Jesus love others with heaven's interest. The Word testifies of God's work through Jesus as the Logos. When we read it, we can testify to God's words firsthand. To love Jesus more is to know and read the Word.

Sometimes that's a challenge. When you read God's Word, do you ever feel as if you're reading the dictionary? Just reading a river of words inked on paper?

I know I have.

Maybe that's because you're reading it with a rake rather than a shovel.

I know I was.

I'm not saying we should stop reading books inspired by the Bible or those that share a deeper revelation. That would be like saying we shouldn't sing a worship song we didn't write or eat food we didn't grow. My library has many books about the Book in it. Many of the titles were recommended to me. Francis Chan, A. W. Tozer, C. S. Lewis, John Piper, James Emery White, and many others have challenged and sparked my faith when it needed to be examined. These authors and many others have two things in common: they breathe oxygen, and they dig deep into God's Word, pointing me to Scripture.

But they dug.

They sold their rake and got a shovel.

I want a shovel.

I want to dig.

Do you?

The Rake and the Rocks

If the season is right where you live, I want you to do something. If not, come back to this page and do the following at a later time. Find a small stone, about the size of a golf ball. Paint it yellow or wrap it in yellow paper, tape, or frosting—somehow make it yellow to represent a gold nugget, a small chunk of valuable truth.

Next, go to your shed, garage, garden, or neighbor's house and get a rake and a shovel.

Now let's take a walk. Bring the yellow rock and garden tools with you.

Find a spot in your yard that's free of utility and sprinkler lines, where it is safe to dig. The front yard is good, although your neighbors might wonder what in the walnut you're doing.

Scoop a hole about six to eight inches deep and wide. Throw the gold-painted rock in the hole. Now bury the pseudo-treasure, pack down the disturbed earth, and to your best ability place your yard back as it was.

The yellow rock is now waiting to be unearthed.

Of the tools you have with you, which is the best one to help you retrieve the rock—the rake or the shovel?

The rake will move dirt…eventually. But the shovel will complete the same task in thirty seconds. The rake is brilliantly designed to scrape a surface, to gather autumn's dry, spent leaves into heaps.

You can rake the Bible your entire life and miss the treasure that lies six inches below the surface. Without the right tools, biblical truth will remain buried like that stone in the yard.

Any book an exhaustive list of authors write, I write, or you write must be supplemental to your spiritual diet. These books must never become the main course. They can push you to a deeper level of understanding and they can educate and encourage you, but you have learn to dig on your own.

We only truly uncover what we search for ourselves.

The yellow rocks are waiting.

So dig.

Vitamin-D Junkies

I live in the world's medical headquarters, near the Mayo Clinic in Rochester, Minnesota. It's a great place to live if you want to be challenged in your faith, as there's never a shortage of people that need to be loved, healed, and prayed for. *And the God I serve heals.*

New studies about medical breakthroughs occur all the time in these parts. For instance, waiting in the lobby for my wife one afternoon, I read an article about the importance of vitamin D to aid in the absorption of calcium. The article explored specific ties, and I won't bore you with the medicinal details. The main point was that calcium works better and goes farther in our bodies when vitamin D is present.

What I appreciate about this relationship is that they partner to make each other more effective. Vitamin D generally comes from the food we eat, but it is primarily absorbed through our skin from the sun. Calcium comes from many sources; the most popular is dairy milk.

You may have seen the commercials.

Got milk?

Books about the Bible are like vitamin D. We take them in, and they enhance the absorption of the Word into our lives and hearts.

Especially if they are directly from the Son.

Books about the Book should accompany the calcium-rich nutrients that can be found in the Word, and we all start with the milk of it.

> Like newborn infants, long for the pure spiritual milk, that by it you may grow up into salvation.
>
> —1 PETER 2:2

A diet high in calcium, correctly absorbed into our bodies with the aid of vitamin D, produces strong bones and a body able to support its own weight and handle increased pressure placed upon it. Then the fastest way to have the calcium absorbed quickly is to move, to put motion to the chemistry.

Our spiritual bodies are no different. A spiritual diet high in the Word, absorbed correctly into our spirits with the help of study resources, produces hearty followers of Christ, able to stand firm in righteousness when the winds of increased pressure blow in. To then put into motion what is being taught is key for the spiritual chemistry as well.

Pseudo: (n) supposed to be but not really so; false; not genuine[1]

Pseudo-masters never completely stand in their own faith because of a weak skeletal system. Their bones are depleted because they are addicted to vitamin D but low on calcium.

They're deficient in the Word.

They're proficient in vitamin D.

They're vitamin-D junkies.

This lack of face-to-face relationship with Jesus and His personal revelation creates a foundational weakness, and pressure will cause a crisis. These pseudo-Jedis need the next book release, the next conference, and the next fix.

Eventually they snap.

Then it's on the news.

Or worse, your family's "front page" or the rumor mill at your school.

When we only know and ingest books about the Book, we sound trendy, hip, and probably add value during whatever conference discussion may be going on at the moment. But at the end of the day, we're just a pseudo-Static Jedi. One who, from outward appearances, may appear to be a master but slowly becomes a vitamin-D dealer.

Think of it this way.

As you have read this book, what parts have you skimmed through?

A personal story of mine?

Maybe.

Or as you have been reading, maybe you glanced over something else.

Time and time again when reading this book based upon the Book, what have you skimmed over?

If you are reading as I used to, you will find yourself skipping over the chunks of scripture quoted.

What does that tell us about how we read and consume His Word?

Measly scanning past the quoted text for God's Word.

The words we skip over and skim are God's words.

Not to make an arrogant assumption, but the ones you possibly highlight or circle with ink are mine.

While I believe what I'm writing is inspired by the Holy Spirit, who is my helper in this process, there is a healthy perspective to keep close.

Here it is.

There is difference in God's words and man's.

Even when reading, we rush to get to the vitamin D and just skim the calcium, the milk of the word.

God knows which ones of us have a balanced diet—those of us who have long-term health and are able to stand, and the others of us who are grasping for the next crutch.

What's crazy is that God can use both.

But His ability does not give me the ability to use crutches.

He wants me to run.

Ditch the crutch.

Environmental Crutch

Two college students from a prominent Christian institution in Minneapolis were sitting across the aisle from me. As we soared through the air, strapped to a metal tube, at five hundred miles per hour, I had some time to people watch. To learn firsthand about what makes people tick. So I watched their first-act performance unfold before my eyes.

Branded on their folders was the name of their school. They laughed, talked, and from the nature of their conversation about mathematical equations appeared intelligent. Shortly after takeoff their conversation took a different turn. They began discussing what they liked to drink, how they usually drink, and, finally, what they were going to drink later in the flight.

As far as planning to get my drink on, I'm usually hoping for club soda with a lime or a coffee when the flight attendant comes my way—except I'm usually passed out with the book I'm reading on the floor three rows back because of late-night-early-morning ministry fatigue that sets in once I'm sitting in one place for longer than fifteen minutes. Drool everywhere. Poor guy in 6-C never saw it coming.

These students were deciding what they were to going to drink before the beverage service even happened. And they were going to do it together—as if to say, "Finally we are free! We can do what we want!"

Since I'm familiar with the school's policies impressed upon the student body, I knew the school desired behavior of its students in contrast to the actions about to transpire.

Let me stop right here and say that I don't want to fully discuss if drinking is sin, not a sin in moderation, not a sin at all, gives the appearance of evil, or causes a brother to stumble. I don't want to discuss whether real wine should be used in Communion because you were raised in a Catholic or Episcopalian faith. I don't want to hear that drinking is culturally not OK unless you live on the United States territory island of St. Croix, nor do I want to debate what *drunk* really means in the Bible or any other arguments I've heard over the years to fit a person's desire-driven stance on the issue.

Whether tatted, gauged, permed, or not, the body—your body and my body—is the temple. (That also applies to cheeseburgers. Too many and we grow from temple to cathedral!)

Take booze totally out of the equation, and there still was something wrong with the math. In that brief moment Jesus gave me a picture—a piece of art—to illustrate what was happening with these two college students. I could see chains wrapped around their wrists and necks.

Shackles.

In need of the master locksmith.

They were chained to their school environment's quest for God. But this quest was not tied to their own. They were not committed to follow the standards outlined by the university as a path to God. Their ability to master the noise was maybe a "had to" rather than a "get to." Their campus served as an environmental insulator for their own spirituality and by its very nature brought balance to their lives.

As long as they stayed on campus.

Or at least between the lines.

None of us are wired to stay within in the lines. Not even from an early age do we desire to color life in the lines. Just look at a four-year-old's art. Venturing outside the bold, black confines of the lines—the law—is in each one of us. We're hardwired to color. Dying to ourselves is not easy.

This isn't to say that the presence of alcohol in a person's life means the absence of God. That's not the point. However, these environments—Christian campuses, churches, exclusive small groups, or ministry initiatives—can easily become places to float around in our own little Christian bubbles. But once outside that scope of positive influence, our ship can sometimes sail in a different direction.

Obvious in the natural and revealed to me in the supernatural, these students were headed in a different direction from the original intention God had for them. These collegiates lived within a setting that provided them with truth on every plate and around every corner. They were required to regularly attend a chapel service (where I had previously spoken) and take Bible classes and Bible tests.

They may have known a lot of things academically, but once they left their Christian habitat, they were in deep water. How would they navigate? What course would they choose?

After their fourth round of booze, I knew Mr. Honesty Beaver had paid both of them a visit and started nibbling on their ear. Boldly I leaned across the aisle and got their attention. Then I asked them the question my sons have asked me countless times about things as simple as making eggs.

"Why?"

The student sitting closest to me repeated the question. In his clouded confusion he thought the question had to do with what he was doing in that moment. What he heard me ask was, "Why drink?" I found that interesting. Was that because he was holding a plastic cup? Or because somewhere deep within he was aware that his actions were in contrast to the code of conduct agreement he had signed with his own hands?

I pointed to the folders stashed in the seat pockets with the motion sickness bags they would need in the morning. "Why did you choose to go to that school?"

With a confused look on his face and a "get rid of this guy" tone, he answered, "Because."

I pushed a little harder. "Seriously. I'm curious. Why do you go to that school? I'd like to know, as I work with a lot of schools like yours."

"It's a good environment," he said.

Environment. There is the why. These guys were using their Christian school as a crutch upon which to prop their spirituality. But here, thousands of miles in the air, they were outside their environment. What could keep them afloat in their faith now? They were on the loose and free to choose outside the confines their normal surroundings dictated.

Sometimes our Christian ponds can be the noise, propping up our spiritual lives with convenient crutches. But what happens when our ability to live a righteous life before the Lord is based upon our outward surroundings or environment? We sink when we step out of the boat. Our focus is captured by all that is bright and shiny and alluring. With our eyes on anything but Jesus, we sink.

Just ask a guy named Peter. This impulsive disciple demonstrated that our ability to stand when the setting leads us to sink is based on standing in Jesus. When no one is watching or with you in the water, a Static Jedi keeps his eyes on the Master.

It's not clear to the pseudo-Static Jedi that righteousness must stand when the setting sinks. Our mastery of the noise cannot be environmentally dependent. The key to mastery is the environment of our hearts. Wherever we journey, we carry our heart's ecosystem with us.

So how does this story end?

Before deplaning, I wrote a note on a piece of paper from my journal, then stood up and handed it to the young man. I wrote what I believe the Holy Spirit was asking me to give to him. The note said:

> Know whatever man has painted, Jesus can make art from anything; any canvas, any mess, yours or mine. The Creator is not done, I beg you to not be as well. I've found mankind and Jesus need never be in the same box. One will always fail you and one will not. Jesus is not accountable for the church's shortcomings, we are. Rise above what people pull you down to be. You can't do this, and that's the point. It's not what we can do. See you in chapel. (Note: You can watch the parts of that note come to life in a completed version that inspired the video Repaint Jesus on my youtube.com/ nooneunderground.)

I could have stayed in my seat like everyone else. However, when others sit, a Static Jedi is found standing—even standing alone, with a message not in hand but secure in heart.

■ INTERNAL INQUIRY ■

1. What are some of your biggest obstacles to shoveling, not raking, God's Word?

2. Are you easily strung out on "vitamin D" in your intake of nutrients in your life with God?

3. What crutches are you standing on?

4. What people or environments bring you down in your pursuit of Jesus?

■ EXTERNAL EXCHANGE ■

1. What does it mean to approach God's Word with a shovel instead of a rake? Are there good resources for this quest? If so, what are they?

2. Have you ever found yourself more compelled to read other books instead of reading the Bible? Why do you think that is?

3. What environments bring you most alive?

4. What sorts of things have you found to be crippling to your faith?

Chapter 7

QUASI-STATIC MASTERS

IT'S THE CLASSIC telephone game. Start with a message and whisper it to the next person. By the time the words have passed through the filter of many people, they rarely resemble the original.

The message gets diluted and changed.

By way of the telephone game, a quasi-Static Jedi imparts God's Word to the next generation. Speaking but not fully mastering what was originally said. Sharing truth without understanding.

Previous generations of true Static Jedis passed the Bible to the next age bracket through a written and oral tradition; however, it's important to note it wasn't a summary of the text or a version of it.

It was the whole text.

Quasi: seemingly; apparently but not really[1]

Jewish boys were required to memorize piles of Scripture. Rabbis that were master Torah teachers knew the entire Torah by memory. Rabbis, as master Torah teachers who taught with *Semikhah*, authority, had the entire Old Testament committed to memory. The journey to this kind of mastery was an intensely difficult one and started at an early age. And it wasn't just Jewish boys who did this, but also other worldviews that, in their early roots, shared an affinity for memorization, discipline, and regimen.

When we wield God's actual words, they never return void.

Ours, on the other hand, do.

Maybe you can relate to this—at times I've not shared a verse with someone because I didn't want to sound cliché or religious. Or religiously cliché. That's hard to admit. But it will be even harder to look Jesus in the face someday and explain why I didn't.

So I'm learning I'd rather be cliché than void.

Wouldn't you?

> So shall my word be that goes out from my mouth; it shall not return to me empty, but it shall accomplish that which I purpose, and shall succeed in the thing for which I sent it.
>
> —Isaiah 55:11

Imagine sitting across the table from someone at work during lunch hour or at church and speaking a life-giving Word to them that has been hidden in your heart. What a privilege! And to do it not for your own glory but to see God's Word move into the core of their being—God's truth precisely and accurately delivered to the right place at the pivotal time. Amazing.

A Static Jedi knows God's Word and is ready to give an answer when one is requested.

> But in your hearts honor Christ the Lord as holy, always being prepared to make a defense to anyone who asks you for a reason for the hope that is in you; yet do it with gentleness and respect.
>
> —1 Peter 3:15

Which would be more effective when addressing stress and worry—telling our own stories or sharing our experiences while powerfully pairing them with sections of Jesus's words *from memory*?

I ask this question because I missed this exact chance, and I wish I could go back in time and share something with someone that I didn't in the moment. A pastor friend of mine was in transition. He was working in a secure position and doing great work in global missions, and he and his wife were expecting a baby. But God had called him to plant a church, and he was wrestling with those familiar questions:

What if?

What next?

It's a natural reaction when God calls us to do something hard or beyond our little security box. I wanted to encourage him with words of life, but without a Bible nearby I simply shared my story and a version of what Jesus said in Matthew 6:

> Therefore I tell you, do not be anxious about your life, what you will eat or what you will drink, nor about your body, what you will put on. Is not life more than food, and the body more than clothing? Look at the birds of the air: they neither sow nor reap nor gather into barns, and yet your heavenly Father feeds them. Are you not of more value than they? And which of you by being anxious can add a single hour to his span of life?
>
> —MATTHEW 6:25–27

Which was fine, but it fell short of the Static Jedi standard.

In my hotel room that night I wrote in my journal: "Tonight I didn't flow and I missed it. I wasn't ready. I was more of a quasi-Static Jedi in the mastery of God's Word. I offered an over-paraphrased version of the truth. Memorize Matthew 6."

Rise of the Paraphrasers

Ever search for a calculator to solve a third-grade math problem? At times I wait for the calculator application to load or paw through the junk drawer in the kitchen to find my special math-making machine. In that amount of time I could have balanced the checkbook twice! I find myself chained to my little digital helper and less reliant on my God-given brain. Thirty-seven minus fourteen? *Hold on. Let me grab my calculator.*

In this digital age we rely on Google or a Bible application on our phones to find God's Word when we need it quickly. All that information is great, and access to it is even better. However, Albert Einstein said, "Information is not knowledge."[2] In God-orchestrated appointments, flowing truth is better than googling.

We will never own truth if it is mere information housed in the digital web for us. The truth must possess us.

God gives a litmus test to know when knowledge begins to hold us:

> You shall therefore lay up these words of mine in your heart and in your soul, and you shall bind them as a sign on your hand, and they shall be as frontlets between your eyes. You shall teach them to your children, talking of them when you are sitting in your house, and when you are walking by the way, and when you lie down, and when you rise. You shall write them on the doorposts of your house and on your gates.
>
> —DEUTERONOMY 11:18–20

Sadly, if we are not confident in God's Word, where true knowledge is found, we can only fire "scripture-ish" ideas at people—biblical concepts loosely mixed with what sounds like an ancient proverb, a revelation birthed in someone else, or just a good saying. Truth becomes a version of the original. Similar, yes, but still different at the core.

Reminds me a bit of gardening actually.

Gardening 101

My wife and I love to garden. Right off our garage on the sunny side of our house we put in a small twelve-by-six-foot garden and have a blast growing things to eat and share. My wife is quite the gardener, and we are doing our best to teach our sons firsthand sowing, reaping, tilling, watering, and what to do when the bunnies eat our spoils.

I have two favorite things to grow. First would have to be these little table grapes found in Minnesota. These tart, pea-sized grapes make great little treasures to drop in a bowl of popcorn if you are going to watch a movie or a football game.

The other family favorite is tomatoes. They're pretty easy to grow, and there's so many ways to enjoy them once they are bright red and juicy—homemade sauces, salsa, soups, and sandwiches all can use this little fruit. Or you can enjoy them straight-up, sliced with salt. Some people eat them like an apple.

When selecting tomatoes to grow, you need to know that not all tomatoes are tomatoes. You call it a *tom-ay-to*, and I call it a *tom-ah-to*. But beyond the various pronunciations of the word, there are also different models of the fruit. There exist a myriad of choices in variety, but the basic stems of each variety come from either heirlooms or hybrids. (Hybrid not in the sense of an internal gas/electric engine but rather the kind of seed contained inside a tomato.)

A hybrid tomato, on the inside, is a stark contrast to the original heirloom. You find two versions on the inside, but the outsides of these tomatoes look the same. And the hybrid tomato is but a version of the original.

When a hybrid seed falls on fertile soil, something happens, yes—but only once. These adapted versions of real seeds produce life for a single season but cannot reproduce in the seasons that follow. Plants grown from the seeds of a hybrid usually do not produce seeds that can grow the same type of plant.

Hybrid seeds are dead inside.

Infertile.

Similarly, when we dilute the Word of God, we offer hybrid seeds. And quasi-Static Jedis use hybrid seeds to plant words of life—but that life is reproduced just once, if that.

On the other hand, open-pollinated, non-hybrid plants

produce seeds that will produce many more plants after their own kind. The seeds grow into plants resembling the plant that originally produced the seed.

Just like a disciple.

Another Static Jedi.

So memorize God's Word, and offer the text itself—not a hybrid version of it. Be an heirloom tomato. The big ugly kind. The most flavorful kind.

Because people like flavor.

 The maker who knit us together in the first place is the only one who can knit us together in the second place.
#staticjedi @ericsamueltimm

Just ask the wedding guests at Jesus's first miracle. He made the most flavorful wine, packed with flavonoids, because He is the most flavorful, flavonoid-packed wine there is. Flavonoids are known for reducing cardiovascular disease—and it should be no surprise to learn that these diseases are the top killers of the human race.

Sickness of the human heart.

Cancer of the human heart.

Blockage of the human heart.

So many heart problems. Natural and supernatural. The world needs Jesus.

We need to get to the heart of each heart issue—and we can't do it. Only the maker can. It's only the maker of the heart that can heal the heart's sickness. The maker who knit us together in the first place is the only one who can knit us together in the second place. Why take our hearts anywhere else? Why try any other wine?

Oh, taste and see that the LORD is good! Blessed is the man who takes refuge in him!

—Psalm 34:8

Taste and see. Taste is a powerful blessing we get to enjoy each day, and I'm reminded of this gift when I eat a creation from the earth that's packed with flavor. Every time you eat something delicious, don't miss the favor in the flavor. That's how God made us to consume the energy we need—through our taste buds, unlike the plants or other creatures that absorb energy and nutrients through their skin or some other monotonous food source.

The Lost Order of They

We get to choose what to eat, and the amazing thing is that it can be different each time. We get to put delicious food that keeps us alive in our mouths and enjoy each bite. The better the food, the higher the octane for our bodies.

But there are some lower-octane food items with a short power boost that occasionally ensnare me with their caloric gaze. One of these traps is found at many festivals and outdoor events where I speak, and it is the mighty and marvelous funnel cake.

If funnel cakes are not in heaven, it's possible I'm going to be a bit disappointed. If we get there and no funnel cakes are to be found, I'll exclaim loudly, "Lord? Hallowed be Your name, but there's a question in the back.... Yeah, I was just wondering, since there's no suffering here, where the funnel cakes are?"

I can just see God looking at me, grinning with a side smirk that sends seven hundred planets flying in the direction of His smile and into the abyss of the cosmos. And He says, "Hold out your hand."

I'll put my hand out...slowly.

God's looking at me, and He can see the excitement in my eyes. He is a God of surprises, and He wants give me a surprise.

Then He says, "Snake Eyes, shut your eyes." (Snake Eyes is my name in heaven—it was the G. I. Joe guy I wanted to be all the time, so just go with me on this one.)

I shut my eyes.

One second passes on the clock of the new earth, but by the clock of the old earth, it's about 86,400,000 seconds.

Then I can feel it in my hand. This crispy, hot, pan-dripped, brown confectionery goodness warms my palm to the tips of my fingers. The spongy flour and sugar collide in a deep-fried batter only to find its final resting place where it belongs: trapped within the cells of my body. The steam gathers below this treasure only to collect in small drops that speak to the rest of my body that the treat train is about to dock at the station.

I open my eyes with great expectation to see the miracle. Only once my eyes lock upon what's in my hand, my smile turns away.

I notice something no one should ever have to notice when holding a hot, fresh funnel cake. *There is no powdered sugar.*

When I eat a funnel cake, I want the dusting of powdered sugar to look like new snow on a winter day with the frozen earth underneath undetectable to the naked eye, covered in an eternally powered hoar frost. With no powdered sugar, a funnel cake loses its magic, like a fairy without fairy dust or a ferry boat that's not a paddle steamer.

Looking up at the Creator of funnel cakes, I complain, much like the Israelites of old: "There's no powdered sugar."

Then God summons an angel over and gives a powerful nod, only to send the seas into a huge wave that would make the Polynesian surfer gods quake with fear. The angel lifts his arms, majestically stretches his wings, and then, in a strange flicking motion, starts running his fingers through the feathers of his wings. A light dust starts falling from heavenly wings.

It's powdered sugar. Powdered sugar from an angel's wings.

And that's where powdered sugar comes from.

Now you know.

(I should note that if the feather-keeper is on vacation, causing production to be low, powdered sugar is made from angels' armpits, like those little dried deodorant balls—you know the ones if you wear deodorant. Or maybe angels don't wear deodorant. If so, I would have to submit that's where brown sugar comes from, then. Now some of you never want to see powdered or brown sugar again, I'm sure!)

Even with this knowledge, I don't want to go without sugar or occasional sweet things.

You may never want to go without food either. So much of our days revolve around it. We eat at holidays, on vacation, every day, and for special occasions. A lot of our activities involve food, and much of the world can't fathom the kind of food we know.

So many of us don't eat because of hunger, but rather out of boredom. Most of us don't even know what hunger is. Yet approximately twenty-five thousand children die each day in a ditch or in their mother's arms because they can't get what many of us don't even have a clue what it's like to go without.[3] They can't get nourishment. Can't pay at window number one and pick it up at window number two. Can't walk into a store and select a clean, safe tomato—whether it be hybrid or heirloom. Don't have the privilege to randomly shuffle over to a large metal box that keeps things fresh longer (aka the fridge).

I catch myself wandering over to it—my grandfather referred to it as "the icebox"—especially at night, making these unnecessary pilgrimages only to do something strange. I open the fridge and stare inside with a longing gaze. Then, with a hopeless sigh, I proclaim, "There's nothing to eat." Even though the shelves contain food and ingredients to make a recipe. The same hopeful journey to the pantry for a snack often plays out the same way.

Some people have little food, and some have much. But no matter our oil-or-water experiences, all people eat food. It's a powerful force that wields a powerful attraction. Even in the Garden of Eden the magic allure of food was too much for Eve.

Then, possibly, the magical allure of a woman's request was too much for Adam.

Food was in the beginning, and food will be in the end and even past the end. It's been a part of human history and will be a part of our future human experiences. Food is bookended, bookmarked, and then bookended again in God's Word through the fall, the redemption of man, and the marriage supper of the Lamb. The meal we'll share at the end of time that's described in Revelation 19 sounds amazing, and I'm looking forward to that banquet. (I'm also hoping funnel cakes are on the menu.)

Food is a big deal.

It's a big deal to us and a big deal to God.

The fall of man started with food, when Adam and Eve ate us out of house and home.

The redemption of man started without it, when Jesus fasted in the wilderness.

The last supper had food on table.

Jesus then took that food and brought it to a new reality and now remembrance.

The celebration will contain it, as we enjoy the marriage supper of the Lamb.

Food is where it all started, and it seems food is where it all ends.

In the Garden of Eden the green light was given to Adam and Eve by God to consume anything they could see, except for this fruit—food from this specific tree.

But we like fruit.

That's why we chase it.

When we chase fruit and lose sight of the vine, we forget that God is a person and that He can be known by more than the fruit He produces in our lives. It's just noise to chase the blessings, not the blesser, the gifts but not the giver.

> Can the wedding guests mourn as long as the bridegroom is with them? The days will come when the bridegroom is taken away from them, and then they will fast.
>
> —MATTHEW 9:15, EMPHASIS ADDED

Look at that verse a bit closer, and then examine yourself as I had to examine myself too. It says that when the bridegroom is taken from them, then they will fast.

Who is the "they" He is speaking about? We are. The bridegroom will come back, but until that time, the Order of They will remain and continue. We don't *have* to fast; we *get* to. When we fast in the natural, something happens in the supernatural. We abstain from food for a spiritual purpose. We go without the distraction of food to get closer to God.

When was the last time you put down food and picked up the Word? Said to Jesus, "I love you more than food. I'm only going to eat as Daniel did or have only water because I want to know and love You more"?

For many, feeding our flesh has kept the flesh man roaring back, challenging our spirit man. That flesh man screams, louder and louder with each generation. For generations of men, the desire to click on pornography is just the same as the desire to eat a chicken sandwich. It's a different type of food, but it's feeding the same flesh. The flesh woman says to generations of women that they're not beautiful, and it's the same flesh woman who desires power over the new creation.

The flesh man or woman shouldn't be in our lives. That flesh must be dealt with once and for all, not simply contained or controlled in sedated form through numbing activities such as eating food. To contain or control the flesh is to let it live in sedation and the way of a quasi-Jedi. A quasi-Static Jedi has forgotten to remove the fruit, or food, altogether in order to chase the vine. In doing so generations of followers of Christ have excluded themselves from the Order of They.

Other worldviews fast far more than you may realize. In an

organized, mandated fashion sometimes based upon fear, generations forgo food to seek what they seek. Jesus, the master who began His ministry by being led by the Holy Spirit to fast, also leads and equips us to continue the ministry He placed in motion.

To die to the flesh is to follow the master.

If Jesus fasted, who are we to say we don't have to? If this was part of the equipping of Jesus, then how important is fasting to equip us to be His followers? Without fasting, the noise can furtively steal in to claim valuable real estate in your soul.

Not from obligation but from opportunity a Static Jedi secretly joins the Order of They. This order brings clarity.

The noise creates mountains.

Prayer and fasting remove them.

Order them to move, as a Static Jedi who is a member of the Order of They would do.

Vending Machine Prayer Lives

Tucking my son in bed is a process that has become quite ordered in his three-year-old mind. He knows that after his bath, we brush his teeth. (I made the mistake one night of forgetting the lotion on his hands and face and was quickly reminded of what Mom does.) Then, after reading his storybook Bible, laced with a few life lessons from Dr. Seuss, it's time to say bedtime prayers.

One night my son asked, "Dad, can I pray?"

"Sure," I said. "You bet."

Xavier began to pray. "Dear Jesus, please bless us this food and give me a good night sleep. Amen."

I smiled and added a few lines of my own, then kissed him on his head and left him to sleep. But my mind started to race as I became challenged by the nature and subject matter of his prayer. The ritual of choosing a bedtime snack from our vending-machine pantry had direct connections to how I was teaching my son to pray. "Please bless" and "give me" were his words. He heard me pray at bedtime, meals, and other times, and what had stuck with him most from my example was making requests of God, not giving reverence to God.

As a father I must do better.

As a son or daughter of God you must inspect how you're praying, as your Father is listening. It's easy to let our prayer lives slip into request sessions with God, but this is the way of a quasi-Static Jedi.

"God, I need this and I want that."

"Please do this or do that."

We further add to this false mastery of the noise when we approach God only when hungry.

Or when we need something.

This has been illustrated at times in my life, when I've only sought God through prayer when tragedy struck or when I needed Him to do something, forgetting to seek Him in prayer when triumph abounded or because of what He had done or simply for who He is.

A pseudo mastery of the noise through prayer mirrors that of a vending machine.

It's not bad to ask our Father for requests or specific blessings. However, Jesus teaches us how to pray, and it's a prayer that begins differently. Most of us know the end of His prayer: *Amen*. But it's easy to forget the beginning.

Jesus, as a son, teaches us how to pray without words of request at the beginning but with words of honor and admission to the heavenly Father:

> Our Father in heaven, hallowed be your name.
> —Matthew 6:9

Hallowed: holy, consecrated, sacred, revered[4]

When our prayer life becomes a mundane task of asking for things before small events and after large tragedies, we live a false mastery. Like approaching a vending machine, we gather up the leftover change, look into heaven's glass, and ask for a Whatchamacallit candy bar while a greater feast awaits.

The feast also becomes named a *what do you call it,* as it is unknown by name to the quasi-Static Jedi. But the feast is known to the master of the static as the table of thanksgiving.

■ INTERNAL INQUIRY ■

1. When have your words failed you?

2. How do your digital devices—even your Bible app—become your crutch?

3. Have you excluded yourself from the Order of They? What do you need to do about it?

■ EXTERNAL EXCHANGE ■

1. Why do you like funnel cakes?

2. What is the hardest thing for you when it comes to memorizing the Word of God?

3. What do you think is the greatest benefit of memorizing the Word?

4. Why is fasting food so difficult?

5. How can we pray for one another?

Chapter 8

NOISY LIVES = NOISY CHURCHES = ?

A LL IT TOOK was a trip to the Philippines for the smoke to clear in my heart. I flew on four different planes to get there, connecting here in the United States, later in Tokyo, and landing in Manila. Eventually my travels by plane, boat, and taxi bike led me to a place where I saw the church being the church. I saw what it looks like to master the noise firsthand as a small collection of followers of Jesus overflowed with love for their community. By the fruit evidenced in their lives, there was no doubt they individually and corporately were in love with Jesus.

But there is much darkness in their own backyard. At a fast-food restaurant I got a front-row seat to see the pain. Two eight-year-old girls sat across from an older gentleman who was clearly not local and not their grandfather. The restaurant bordered a red-light district—a place of child slavery. Kid's meals sat in front of the girls. These were someone's daughters. At a crowded restaurant their blank stares cut through the noise. Their silent, wounded expressions screamed loudly to me.

I've never been so angry, so hurt, so frustrated, and so compassionate at one time. I wept bitterly for the girls and asked Jesus to help me love the old man as He does. From this experience I will continue to challenge a generation to understand this truth: this scene is where pornography leads. The journey begins with a click of a computer mouse when no one is looking.

It leads to believing you can own another person for your own pleasure. When the who becomes a what, we become who we are not meant to be.

Thankfully the bookend experiences to this one included joyful moments with new friends. I enjoyed home-cooked meals and a long afternoon of conversation with the pastors of a local church that borders a community nicknamed by locals as a "place of death" or "death city."

The huge development of this "death city" was built upon ritualistic burial sites. These people had nowhere to go, so they started building on top of a cemetery. Imagine your living room with a coffin in the center. Then picture three or four headstones in your bedroom with people buried right below you. Oh, and when it rains, everything rises, so there might be a floater or two. Sounds like something out of a movie, I know, but this is real life for people of this earth we both stand on. Same dirt, same sun. They're just farther away from our subdivisions and neighborhoods.

On a December afternoon during my visit the pastors and a few others were going to visit a few church members who lived in this place of death. Before we ventured through the ironclad gates, we huddled for a few words and prayer. One of the pastors explained the dangers we could encounter.

"The place we are going is very dangerous, and you possibly could be robbed or hurt," he said in his Tagalog English. "If someone corners you or threatens your life with a weapon like glass, a cutter stick, or a gun, don't be afraid. Just say the word *a-lin-ce*."

And then we prayed.

But wait. What was that last word? My mind got stuck on the words I did catch—*robbed, hurt, threatens your life.*

So after the pastor had finished praying, I raised my sweaty palm. "Pastor, what was that last word we are to say? I want to make sure I got it down."

He repeated the word, this time slower and drawn out for my comprehension. *"Alliance."*

"What does that word mean?" I asked. "'I come in peace' or 'I mean no harm'?"

The pastor smiled. "No, Eric. It's far simpler than that."

Time stood still as I waited for the explanation. I would pull these words of freedom into my ears and bury the sounds deep within my vocabulary.

He turned and pointed to a small sign hung high behind us. Just like a volunteer caught on stage at a Jared Hall magic show, I looked where he pointed.

A hand-painted sign read "Alliance."

He explained, "It's the name of our church."

Alliance.

Successful Bodies, Not Buildings

Followers of Christ are the church. The church is not a brick-and-mortar structure. Or made of grass and bamboo. The church is made of flesh and blood. And our ability to master the noise as individuals will directly affect the measure of corporate impact we have on our cities and this world.

And here's the thing. We measure church success differently in America than churches do around the world. Good video and media teams, sexy lights, stunning graphics, and excellent programs—these are our standards of success. Now none of these things are bad in and of themselves, and when used correctly they can be great tools to reach people. It's all to do with a search for relevance.

The word *relevant*, other than being the name of a great magazine, is another word for *effective*. So you can be effective with all that technology, and you can be effective with an overhead projector and a ukulele. Everything depends on the audience and tribe you're trying to reach.

But let me ask you these questions that have forever redefined what "church success" means to me. Can you walk into the deadest parts of your town and, when threatened at gunpoint for your earthly belongings, just speak the name of your church and, because of how you have loved Jesus corporately and individually in your town, watch the thief withdraw the weapon? Has your community experienced love from you in such a way that by simply speaking the name of the church, you have a covering and no harm befalls you?

This kind of love demands mastery of the noise.

This kind of love does not dance under the clutter but rises above and outpaces death itself.

Take a look at an example of this kind of love, taken from an entry in my Moleskine journal dated December 2, 2011:

> Today I visited an entire town built upon a cemetery, upon death. Some of the living walked around this town, down, as dead. Death was upon them, held them, and shown darkly upon their face. The dead possibly had life, I don't know the past. I cannot see through the smell of death. The dead had nowhere else to go but to a place where the past lays.
>
> The past lays still.
>
> I could hear the dead telling me without words, "The past is always moving just in front of us, out running us, always displaying death to us, and the dead out living us." Surrounded by decay, they built the foundations of their homes on death. In a place that smells of death, looks like death, and is named death. Dreams that died, hopes never fulfilled, and love that was put to death, all exist here. Love that was sent to the grave is no longer even a memory.
>
> Death is the currency that everyone is rich in. A trade that takes life and gives death in exchange. With each transaction, once again they, the dead, bow to the power of the grave. But then I see a name written, but I feel that name spoken. This is the Name. This is a Name that has conquered both death and the grave. A Name who is

building a new home from the ashes of death. A Name who unleashes new dreams, a Name that builds hope and has and will and is displaying love. A Name that makes the dead inside, alive again. Death has no place where this name is in its place...That name is not death, that name is not the grave, that name is not under any other name. That name is Jesus. You carry that Name. We carry that Name to outshine the dark.

I want to be a part of *that* church. I want to better carry *that* name of Jesus. How about you?

 The things that pull the church from its purpose are found in the foundations of the noise. #staticjedi @ericsamueltimm

This won't happen if we're living as slaves to the noise. But when followers of Christ strive to master the noise, this dream becomes a reality for our churches and our gatherings of believers. I hope when you read the Gospels and the New Testament, you're challenged by what your church and my church can to grow into. I hope you'll be encouraged by what we're doing on this earth. If Christ is the head of the church and we are the body, let's be a body filled with disciples that master the noise.

On this note let me say that I get weary of the tiresome church-bashing that takes place. Certainly there are things that are broken and crooked in our churches. But God uses the broken and the crooked to fix and make things straight. He doesn't call us to be perfect. He calls us to be in relationship and to trust Him. He has not asked us to judge but to love.

The things that pull the church from its purpose are found in the foundations of the noise. The noise distorts the outcome of the church. But we can break through to bedrock. We can base our foundation upon the Rock.

Yes, the collected church meets in a building with an address we call the church. But each of us *is* the church. The church is made up of us. Before we continue to look at what's wrong with the church, let's look at what's wrong with us.

Are we made of noise, or are we becoming more like Jesus? We can't do it alone—nor do we have to. Jesus changes us, and the Holy Spirit guides us. "Be not angry that you cannot make others as you wish them to be, since you cannot make yourself as you wish to be," said Thomas á Kempis.[1]

The more we have of Jesus, the greater the love we have; the greater the love, the greater the sacrifice; the greater the sacrifice, the more we become like Jesus; and the more we become like Jesus, the more successful our local churches become.

This process requires the proper investment of time.

A Way to Split Time

My time on the trip had come to a close, and I was headed home on a few different planes. Returning from this journey, I sat in the airplane trying to put my heart back into my body. My brain was now wrestling firsthand with the stark differences between being a Christian and being a disciple.

I had just walked with disciples.

And it was mind-blowing and life-changing.

As I sat there processing all God was showing me, another bomb went off inside me. I was in the air traveling from Japan to the United States, on December 7, 2011, being served and cared for in a peaceful and timely fashion. The above-and-beyond expectations of hospitality customary in the East is a dramatic contrast from the hospitality standards in the West.

I flipped through a magazine, and an ad caught my eye. It was advertising vacation trips to Hawaii. That's when the inner explosion happened. Panicked, my mind raced, putting the pieces together, second-guessing and then reguessing. I was flying to the United States in a commercial jet that took off from Japanese soil, which stood in stark contrast to a flight that took the same journey seventy years earlier to the date. December 7, 1941, had a much different ending than my landing would hopefully have, but it had an eerily similar starting point. Google the date if you need to. I did, just to be sure.

Everyone thinks of changing the world but no one thinks of changing himself.[2]

—Leo Tolstoy

A lot has changed since then. That tragic event, for both sides of the bullets, was the catalyst that brought to the world significant change. It was the snowball kicked down the hill, rolling and picking up momentum until it became the atomic bomb.

Shortly after Pearl Harbor projects developing the atomic bomb achieved success, and this altered everything. The world's history could possibly be divided into "BAF" and "AAF" on a timeline—before atomic fusion and after atomic fusion. The creation of the atomic weapon is the source of many global conflicts, tensions, and peacekeeping challenges today.

The presence of the nuclear bomb continues to shape the future. But in comparison to the change Jesus brought to this earth and to every individual who inhabits the planet, the nuclear threat is a small bullet. The fact of the matter is, history is *not* labeled BAF and AAF on a timeline. The world's calendar is *not* quantified to end where the Mayan calendar stopped, or you wouldn't be reading this book. Instead, it's labeled BC and AD—before Christ and after Christ (*anno Domini*).

What Jesus did, how He lived, what He fulfilled, and what He promised to do changed humanity. It started with a handful of disciples taught firsthand by Jesus, and because of that moment, you're holding that book.

He changed everything. He continues to change everything.

From a long line of Roman, Julian, and Gregorian calendars, history is hinged on eras divided and based upon the conception or birth of Jesus. His life was that huge.

Some have since changed the abbreviations that marked our calendars for thousands of years. The newer "BCE" and "CE" stand for "Before the Common Era" and "Common Era," in place of BC and AD. They omitted Christ from the dating system to comply with political correctness.

I understand why some would want to do this, and my job is to love them.

The changers of the calendar are right anyway. They still split the timeline based on when Jesus walked upon the earth; they just renamed it. *A rose is still a rose.*

Besides, I kind of like it. In Christ we *are* living in a common era. Where God communed with a specific people group, Israel, before Christ, after Christ He began to commune with all people—Jew and Gentile. So, thanks for the change, history date calendar people. Keep it up! You're doing great.

What Jesus did and how He lived may be labeled "common" on a timeline, but the event—the establishment of an intimate relationship between God and man—will forever be extraordinary.

The world has made a distinction.

Have you?

If so, how much different does your life look before Christ and after Christ?

Specifically when it comes to mastering the noise and protecting the time to do so?

This was a haunting question for me.

Everything from behavior, my mind, and my investment of time should be changing to how Jesus would have me function, think, and respond.

Too often those time lines get blurred on the history of our lives.

In a new era being found in Christ in the spiritual but in the physical I find myself living in the old. All while disregarding holiness as legalism and further blurring those lines.

The apparent differences should continue to list themselves as we continue to seek to be like Him, not like who we want or used to be. In this case—a distinction between two eras, one with the noise and one in mastery of it.

Will you draw the line?

The distinction on your timeline will be found in your journey to master the static. Jesus helps us master the noise through the example of what He did and flowing from how He lived. Out of this we make better churches that bear fruit. What we do is a by-product of how we live. How we live is a product of what we choose. What we choose is up to us—choosing the noise or choosing Jesus.

Let's look to Jesus to learn how to master the noise. Fall in love with Jesus.

More.

Again.

Today.

And fall out of love with the noise.

When we possess a passionate love for Jesus, the noise possesses less of us. As we foster that love, we grow more disinterested in the noise and more attracted to Christ. We separate from distractions and mediocrity like oil from water.

■ INTERNAL INQUIRY ■

1. What's your personal version of church success?

2. What does the timeline of your life look like? What are the changing events?

3. What does "Everyone thinks of changing the world but no one thinks of changing himself" mean for you, your life, and your church? Where does change start for you and your church?

4. Is there a difference between being a Christian and being a disciple? Which one are you?

■ EXTERNAL EXCHANGE ■

1. What does your church's version of success look like?

2. Why do you think so many people have negative feelings about church?

3. How do we fall in love with Jesus and out of love with the noise?

Chapter 9

THE STATIC MASTER (PART 1): JESUS ROSE EARLY AND WITHDREW

EVER HAVE THOSE days when you wake up late? Hit the snooze button a few too many times? I used to more frequently than I do in my current season of life with two kid alarm clocks. They did not come equipped with a snooze button!

But tell me if you can relate to this. When I would get up late, or as late as possible, my day would start in a rush. One minute I'm lying prone, my head solid on my pillow. Then, when the absolute last second arrives, I bound up, hurrying from bed to shower. Or maybe skip the shower. Then I'd grab something for breakfast and be out the door and on to my day.

It's easy to become distracted from God by a list of a hundred possible reasons. But starting the day uncentered like this usually left me feeling off-balance for a large part of the rest of it.

I have since learned that mornings are a beautiful time for beautiful things. And believe me, I wouldn't have ever considered myself a morning person! There are all other labels I would place upon myself before "morning person." I am a follower of Christ, husband, father, and Netflix subscriber. As a father, my kids, aka little alarm clocks, would require my attention in the early hours. However, vocationally as a communicator, author, artist, teaching pastor, and adjunct professor, my schedule doesn't usually demand that I get up at 5:30 a.m. as other responsibilities or vocations would.

For years I would just sleep in because I was tired. At least that is what I kept saying in my soul. The issue wasn't hours of sleep. It was an issue of the flesh. I justified my laziness with a collection of different phrases:

- "I'm not a morning person."

- "I'll shower fast and brush my teeth at the same time, and skip breakfast."

- "I can just stay up really late tonight and get it done then."

Constantly hitting the snooze button like daggers to my awaiting life-given day.

Then I looked in the mirror, took an evaluation of myself, and understood what was going on. I was missing the moments. It was a simply profound moment.

I'll ask you to look in the mirror and examine your own daggers.

They could be killing your life, or at least holding you from missing it.

Morning's Blank Canvas

Henry David Thoreau wrote, "The morning wind forever blows, the poem of creation is uninterrupted; but few are the ears that hear it." He says, "[Awake] to a higher life than we fell asleep from.... Morning is when I am awake and there is dawn in me."[1]

Thoreau got it right. The morning is a beautiful experience. It is a sublime gift God gives us every day, freely available for those who will wake and receive it. Those who have the discipline to do it are rewarded. We get to be in a place to hear the poem of creation.

Jesus knew this way before Thoreau penned it. And the

disciples knew this about Him firsthand, as they often woke and caught Him up early. They'd rise and find Jesus with His hair already combed, teeth already brushed, and all twelve little brown sack lunches made and set out in a row.

 The morning is a beautiful experience. It is a sublime gift God gives us every day, freely available for those who will wake and receive it. #staticjedi @ericsamueltimm

Sometimes they'd catch Him in prayer:

> And rising very early in the morning, while it was still dark, he departed and went out to a desolate place, and there he prayed.
> —MARK 1:35

We get a glimpse of Jesus here, up before it's light outside. He seeks and finds a solitary place. If you have kids, you can relate to the desire for finding such a solitary place sometimes—and Jesus's disciples sure acted as children occasionally! Scholars way smarter than I am argue that these young men were ten to twenty years of age, so maybe Jesus really did need to get out of the house and away from the kids before the chaos started.

The word for "early" in this passage refers to the fourth watch of the night, which ran from 3:00 a.m. until 6:00 a.m.

That's early.

Then in the Book of Luke we find people coming out early in the morning to hear Jesus teaching at the temple:

> And every day he was teaching in the temple, but at night he went out and lodged on the mount called Olivet. And early in the morning all the people came to him in the temple to hear him.
> —LUKE 21:37–38

For people to be there early to hear Jesus, He would need to have gotten there already too.

Then John pens that Jesus was up early, ready to do what He was asked to do by the Father:

> Early in the morning he came again to the temple. All the people came to him, and he sat down and taught them.
>
> —JOHN 8:2

Question.

Yes, Dwight? (That was an *Office* reference, in case you didn't catch it.)

If Jesus was coming to an arena or venue in your town and He was going to be there at 5:00 a.m., would you go?

Most of us would go. Even people who don't know and love Him would go. No doubt I would be there to hear firsthand from Jesus. All I'd have to do is show up. That's a no-brainer.

Well, the arena or venue could be closer than you think. Maybe it's your kitchen table before dawn. All you have to do is show up. Showing up is key. And yes, it comes with a cost.

> Just as day was breaking, Jesus stood on the shore; yet the disciples did not know that it was Jesus.
>
> —JOHN 21:4

Post resurrection we see Jesus up early again. After everything had changed, He was up as the day was breaking.

If you look through centuries of church history, you will find that most heroes of the faith consistently woke before the sun. Can you recall one who slept late? Hit the snooze button repeatedly? Followers of Jesus have risen early—even Jesus Himself rose early, as we've already seen—probably all at a cost. But this simple discipline of the Static Jedi empowered their lives to rise above the noise.

In his book *Power Through Prayer* E. M. Bounds expounds on just how early some followers of Christ began their day.

Charles Simeon rose at 4:00 a.m.

John Wesley began at 4:00 a.m.

Bishop Asbury said, "I propose to rise at four o'clock as often as I can."

Samuel Rutherford rose at three in the morning.

Joseph Alleine rose at 4:00 a.m.[2]

That list starts with Jesus, just as the Common Era we live in begins with Jesus. We are invited to begin the day early with Him. You know He is already up and waiting for you.

A Static Jedi rises early to hear the song of creation. Mornings possess a centered stillness that is only found on a new canvas.

The planet Venus is known as the Morning Star because it is the dominant cosmic object in the morning sky, exceeded only by the brightness of the moon. Revelation 22:16 says "I, Jesus, have sent my angel to testify to you about these things for the churches. I am the root and the descendant of David, the bright morning star."

How did Jesus know this to make this illustration about Himself?

Interesting to me that Jesus says He is like Venus.

Speaking without words to my heart,

"Meet with Me before daybreak, before your day figuratively breaks.

Snaps in two,

or compounds into shattered pieces,

too endless to count.

Let's meet before that chaos begins."

As if Jesus continues,

"See that little planet next to the moon,

you see it clearly most in the morning. Well... I'm like that. I'm always there, throughout the day and night but clear in the still of the morning

because you are still,

in the morning.

So be still in the morning."

Maybe it is simpler, and He just spent a lot of mornings looking at Venus,

only this time from the perspective of the earth, not the heavens.

Change your perspective.

Come to a low place where kings are made.

See Venus as the master did from the earth, bright in the morning.

A Static Jedi simply rises early.

Arises early for a purpose. Many purposes. One purpose is to master the art of solace and withdrawal. To speak and listen in prayer.

Withdraw to Draw

The holidays can be those times of the year when people constantly surround us. This immersion around other humans, however, is not just limited to a seasonal occasion. Life continues throughout the year, and life includes people.

There are many different types of people.

Go to a mall or an airport and people watch to illustrate my point.

You could look out at your church's crowd and see the same view you find in the airport. One of the charms of the church is that it is filled with people who have no other reason for their lives to intersect.

A gathering of different shapes, colors, creeds, and tongues.

Varying social standings, educations, experiences, health, age, and economic status.

Dog lovers, cat lovers, cowboys, surfers, bikers, receptionists, doctors, lawyers, teachers, clerks, judges, politicians, conservatives, moderates, and liberals.

Looks a lot like a rehearsal for heaven when every tribe from every nation gathers!

I'm thankful the Holy Spirit sent by Jesus gives community where there would not be unity. The Holy Spirit picks up where we leave off.

Without the Spirit's work in our lives, we can be ugly people.

For me, without the Holy Spirit's fruit of patience and self-control, spending Christmas with thirty-three nieces and nephews would land me in a padded room somewhere where a kind nurse in white shoes brings me something soft to eat.

Some people tend to be introverted, focused inwardly and recharging through time alone. Others are extroverts who focus externally on the world and seek out company. Both styles are self-focused but in a different fashion.

I lean toward the extrovert side of the cosmic personality swing. Maybe that has helped me accomplish what God has me to do. It's certainly made withdrawing from people a challenge! It's made reading a challenge too.

An extrovert looks at a stack of books and sees a stack of papers, while an introvert looks at that same stack and sees a soothing source of escape. An extrovert, when alone, is lonely, while an introvert enjoys the respite of peace and quiet when being alone.

"Everyone wants peace," he says, "but very few care for the things that produce it."[3]

—Thomas à Kempis

Thank God for the Holy Spirit, who shapes both introverts and extroverts, both oil and water! A life with the Spirit's assistance can take an extrovert and help him isolate in helpful, meaningful ways. The Holy Spirit also moves the introvert outside, widening her horizons.

On one side of the pendulum we can be so extroverted, so focused on people and external affairs, that we burn ourselves into exhaustion. We get caught in a schedule of endless hours of service, and the relationships that support us get pushed to the "later" category. Dreadfully the relationships that are our first responsibility get tossed away in place of the mission—the work—we are attending to do. We get so hurried that we never catch ourselves.

> The other tendency is to thoroughly popularize the ministry. He is no longer God's man, but a man of affairs, of the people.[4]
>
> —E. M. BOUNDS

On the other side of the pendulum we can be so introverted that we become cave people and shut out the world so we only have to pray and seek God. Like a holy hermit, we shut ourselves off from men to be open with God alone. To this Bounds says, "We shut ourselves to our study, become students, bookworms, Bible worms, sermon makers...but the people and God, where are they?"[5]

Both are out of balance and out of step with the master. The cadence of a Static Jedi is not one surrounded by an endless string of people or endless hours spent in silence and prayer. It must be about both. Prayer *and* people.

> To live without speaking is better than to speak without living. For the former who lives rightly does good even by his silence, but the latter does no good even when he speaks. When words and life correspond to one another they are together the whole of philosophy.[6]
>
> —ISIDORE OF PELUSIA

Dietrich Bonhoeffer says in *Life Together:*

> Let him who cannot be alone beware of community....Let him who is not in community beware of being alone...each by itself has profound pitfalls and perils. One who wants

fellowship without solitude plunges into the void of words and feelings, and one who seeks solitude without fellowship perishes in the abyss of vanity, self-infatuation, and despair.[7]

Dietrich's master, Jesus, used this private discipline of withdrawal and prayer to focus on the public with great stamina. We catch Jesus, multiple times, locked within the pages of the Gospels, balancing the noise of His time with prayer, isolating from others while seeking the Father. But He didn't remain isolated, nor did He ignore the Father's work on earth. Hand in hand, private and public concerns grow in us.

Jesus lived this.

A Static Jedi will too.

In our previous passage from in Mark 1:35 Jesus left the house and found a solitary place to pray. The word used for *solitary place* here is not a coffee shop. It's solitary, lonely, and uninhabited. It's a desert, an uncultivated region fit for pasturage. It's a hillside or a mountain or the woods. We probably can't all find a patch of woods, but here we find Jesus doing something He does again and again: finding a private place to pray.

Maybe He did this intentionally, removing the comforts of a better-suited solitary place to sit in the raw surroundings of creation and close the gap while seeking the Creator. Adam and Eve sitting in the garden, surrounded by creation, communed with God quite well. There is something about nature that speaks.

Creation is the vocal chords of God speaking each day through the colors of the sunrise, the vastness of the night sky, the teeming of life in the ocean, the majesty of the mountains. Jesus withdraws time and time again to creation to find stillness to pray and seek the Father.

> And after he had dismissed the crowds, he went up on the mountain by himself to pray.
>
> —MATTHEW 14:23

> In these days he went out to the mountain to pray, and all night he continued in prayer to God.
>
> —LUKE 6:12

> Now it happened that as he was praying alone.
>
> —LUKE 9:18

> Now Jesus was praying in a certain place.
>
> —LUKE 11:1

My favorite section about this is found in Mark 6, where this rest and withdrawal occur in the midst of a chaotic time.

We pick up with the crew after Jesus was with His hometown crowd. Maybe He was hoping for a hometown welcome, only to find people were offended with Him at every move. Their unbelief escalated to the point where Jesus "wondered at their unbelief." Jesus then sends out the Twelve with nothing but basic instructions, and they go out and do what He instructed to "many people." Then King Herod cuts off John the Baptist's head and the disciples give Jesus a report of everything they had done.

Ever have days like that? Where it's one big development after another? How did Jesus respond?

> And he said to them, "Come away by yourselves to a desolate place and rest a while." For many were coming and going, and they had no leisure even to eat. And they went away in the boat to a desolate place by themselves.
>
> —MARK 6:31–32

In other words, "Come on, guys. Let's refocus here. There is a lot going on, and we need a break." But they didn't get quite the rest they hoped to find:

> Now many saw them going and recognized them, and they
> ran there on foot from all the towns and got there ahead
> of them. When he went ashore he saw a great crowd, and
> he had compassion on them, because they were like sheep
> without a shepherd. And he began to teach them many
> things.
>
> —MARK 6:33–34

Next, the feeding of the five thousand takes place. From just a Long John Silver's value box of five loaves and two fish, five thousand—and possibly more like ten thousand—people are fed.

But here's the thing.

Jesus wasn't withdrawing from people to give them less.

He was drawing nearer to the Father to give them *more*.

This is the way of the Static Jedi.

The Imitation of Christ by Thomas à Kempis, authored hundreds of years ago in the 1400s, speaks about our struggle with noise. "Everyone wants peace," he says, "but very few care for the things that produce it."[8] Such true words, written well before the pace of life that surrounds us—before electric garage door openers, garage doors, *and* the garage. And well before you could "like" a garage door company on Facebook!

I submit that the noise has been here since the fruit tree in the garden had a piece go missing. Jesus came to seek and save that which was lost.

That missing piece.

The Static Jedi finds the peace in the midst of the missing piece by mastering the noise, and this happens by withdrawing from the noise just as Jesus did. Jesus used the quiet place of prayer and stillness for the solid foundations of the public places in practice.

So shall a Static Master.

We do as the master has done.

A Static Jedi escapes to pray.

■ INTERNAL INQUIRY ■

1. What is it about Jesus's life that challenges you?

2. Are you a morning person or a night person? Is this an excuse or a fact?

3. What are some of the advantages of spending time with Jesus in the morning?

4. Are you afraid of being alone? If so, why do you think that is?

■ EXTERNAL EXCHANGE ■

1. What happens to Jesus's daily canvas as the days get later?

2. Through the lens of Jesus's life, what kind of "solitary places" could we try to find?

3. With Jesus as our model, how does Jesus's habit of waking early and spending time with the Father affect how we should live?

Chapter 10

THE STATIC MASTER (PART 2): JESUS MEMORIZED GOD'S WORD

I'M AMAZED AT how many things I have forgotten in my life. It's mind-boggling. At least I think it is—I can't remember.

For instance, I like nature shows. The BBC produces awesome art in the form of film documentaries. My favorites include *Planet Earth, Human Planet,* and *The Last Lions,* and the list grows longer after each one I watch. If you haven't seen any of them, though, I suggest watching them with Creation goggles, as some of the rhetoric can be based on the assumption of a billion-year-old earth that slothfully evolves, or at least blends, into your Creation world.

You can catch these shows on TV occasionally, but be warned: do not to get sucked into a *Sasquatch Hunter* show! You will watch it to the end thinking it's the episode where they'll actually show you Bigfoot. It's happened to me.

Lastly, I wish I knew how to type the wild call of the Yeti, as I would most definitely add it to my book right here: _____ . Years have passed, and I am still a *Harry and the Hendersons* fan. Good times.

Nature documentaries are a learning and entertainment experience for me. So because of this they make a great gift for me. Recently, a few weeks before Christmas, my family was asking what I would like. After the back-and-forth banter of "I don't want or need anything," I conceded and started to think of a few random items I would like to hang on my office wall. Random dream gifts crossed my mind, the list of which included a T-Rex tooth, hand-written letters from Lincoln and C. S. Lewis, or a really old handwritten Bible.

However, I knew my mother would need a more economical—notice the word *cheap* is not used in this sentence—and readily available solution for our modest gift exchange. So I thought of a few nature documentaries I had not seen or did not own.

Then it hit me. The movie *Frozen Planet* would be a great suggestion. I wanted to see it. There had been a few positive reviews on the piece. I thought it would be a notable addition to my library. Living in Minnesota, it might feel a bit like I was watching a home video, but I was ready for the adventure to begin.

So we exchanged gifts. I got my mother these awesome little personal pie tins and hoped she would make me one or four. (Have we discussed pie? I like pie a lot.) Then I opened my gift and got what I asked for. The wrapping parted, and *Frozen Planet* appeared.

A day or two later I set it up to watch with my family on a holiday afternoon. But about six minutes into the feature, I realized something—I had seen it before.

About six days later during my yearly office-cleaning project to start the new year right, or at least organized, I found it. Not this year's gift. The other copy. I had purchased it from Goodwill months prior. I had bought it, watched it, and forgot all about it.

I possessed the program, but the program did not possess me.

It was head knowledge and had not yet transferred to the lockable chambers of my heart. The information hadn't traveled to my heart and lodged there.

The path from the head to the heart is a small journey that takes effort. It's a feat that directs our feet, where we walk, and what we choose. Once this journey of approximately twenty inches is achieved, the information changes. It ceases to be a measly collection of zeroes and ones that calculate simple data and instead transforms into deoxyribonucleic acid that is used in the development and functioning of all known living organisms.

It becomes a part of our DNA.

So it is with God's Word. We can possess a Bible, but it may not possess us. God's Word must become heart knowledge, a part of who we are.

This is the way of the Static Jedi.

 The path from the head to the heart is a small journey that takes effort. It's a feat that directs our feet, where we walk, and what we choose.
#staticjedi @ericsamueltimm

David echoed the importance of this long ago when he treasured, hid, laid up, and stored God's Word in his heart. Look for yourself in Psalm 119:

> How can a young man keep his way pure? By guarding it according to your word. With my whole heart I seek you; let me not wander from your commandments! I have stored up your word in my heart, that I might not sin against you.
> —PSALM 119:9–11

In David's heart, not his head, was the Word. He hid God's Word in his heart not so he could keep it, but so it could keep him.

Striving to his level, we must know the Word too.

After all, that's also what our master did.

The Art of Knowing the Word

Jesus knew the Word to a level of mastery few will obtain but all can seek. He quoted the Word from memory time and again throughout the Gospels to accomplish what needed to be done in a given moment.

As one example, when Jesus was in the wilderness, being tempted, He responded with Scripture to the devil's attempts to twist God's words. The dialogue is forever captured in Matthew 4:1–11:

> Then Jesus was led up by the Spirit into the wilderness to be tempted by the devil. And after fasting forty days and forty nights, he was hungry. And the tempter came and said to him, "If you are the Son of God, command these stones to become loaves of bread."
>
> But he answered, "It is written, 'Man shall not live by bread alone, but by every word that comes from the mouth of God.'"
>
> Then the devil took him to the holy city and set him on the pinnacle of the temple and said to him, "If you are the Son of God, throw yourself down, for it is written,
>
> "'He will command his angels concerning you,' and 'On their hands they will bear you up, lest you strike your foot against a stone.'"
>
> Jesus said to him, "Again it is written, 'You shall not put the Lord your God to the test.'" Again, the devil took him to a very high mountain and showed him all the kingdoms of the world and their glory. And he said to him, "All these I will give you, if you will fall down and worship me." Then Jesus said to him, "Be gone, Satan! For it is written,
>
> "'You shall worship the Lord your God and him only shall you serve.'"
>
> Then the devil left him, and behold, angels came and were ministering to him.

When Jesus responds each time with "It is written," He's not pulling out a Bible application on His iPhone and conducting a quick word search for His rebuttal to the devil. No, His devotion to the words of God ran much deeper than googling information.

In the Book of Matthew alone Jesus quotes the Hebrew Bible at least thirty-eight times. In fact, much of the twenty-eight chapters in Matthew record Jesus referencing the Word from memory for the need of the moment.

He knew the Word.

By memory.

It was deep within the lockable chambers of His heart, not surfing the surface of the lockless chasm of the mind.

His mastery of the Word began long before the moment Jesus came face-to-face with the devil. Luke captures Jesus at a young age investing time in the temple, the Harvard of its day, a place of instruction and learning. Jesus is asking questions beyond His years, and this learning included listening to other master Torah teachers. Luke further glances at Jesus, the child, and sees Him increasing in wisdom. Translated literally, Luke says Jesus was "increasing in the knowledge of God."

Maybe Jesus didn't just get a free pass to know His Father's words. Maybe He didn't come to the earth in the manger pre-programmed for the matrix. The "fully God" part of His being would know everything, but the "fully man" part would have to strive to memorize and learn. The man, like us, would have needed to train. The desire is supernatural but carried out in the natural.

Either way, where would anyone on this earth, including Jesus, go to learn the knowledge of God through words?

The answer is a hotel drawer.

No, I don't mean a TV remote.

In a lot of hotel drawers you can find a Bible. That's as far as you need to look—in a Bible.

There are swords in hotel drawers.

Think about this every time you stay in a hotel. You have a choice to grab the sword or the remote.

Reach for the sword in the drawer, and let the remote lie; it's probably really dirty anyway.

There were far fewer hotel drawers in Jesus's time, which led many to the temple, where you could find the Torah and the Tanakh. The first five books of the Bible are known as the Torah. The Tanakh is most like the Old Testament found in your Bible.

Now, Jesus was a rabbi. A teacher of the Torah and the Tanakh.

However, Jesus was a not just any teacher in His day. He was a master Torah teacher. Here's how I know. One of the criteria for a master Torah teacher is mastery of the Torah. That's not mastery in the sense of knowing it really well. It's mastery far beyond having a vast library of resources or access to the Internet to help you know it better. It's mastery along the lines of having the entire first five books of the Bible memorized. One would know the entire Torah by memory to be awarded the badge of master Torah teacher.

Grab your Bible and hold in your hand the books of Genesis, Exodus, Leviticus, Numbers, and Deuteronomy. That's a lot to memorize—over seventy-five thousand words, depending on the translation you're holding. My little small print Bible amounts to two hundred fifty-plus pages that Jesus would have known by heart.

By memory.

Bible memorization is absolutely fundamental to spiritual formation. If I had to...choose between all the disciplines of the spiritual life, I would choose Bible memorization...because Bible memorization is a fundamental way of filling our minds with what they need.[1]

—Dallas Willard

But Jesus didn't stop there. There were master Torah teachers, and then there was another level of master Torah teachers altogether—master Torah teachers who taught with *Semikhah*, or authority. This short list of teachers is traced through history back to Moses, and their stature in this part of the world at that time was far beyond that of an elected president or betrothed queen today. The criteria for gaining status as a master Torah teacher with authority was complete mastery of the Tanakh— mastery, in our previous definition, being the complete memorization of the Torah, as well as the remaining books in the Tanakh.

Grab your Bible again.

Hold up the Torah section—Genesis through Deuteronomy.

Now add into your hand Joshua through Malachi.

That's a lot to memorize. The task is a lifelong commitment. It would be around seven hundred thousand words to memorize. The dedication required for such a feat is dumbfounding—but Jesus certainly lived a life that defied logic.

Jesus was a master Torah teacher who taught with authority. In the context of what was required to be this type of rabbi, Jesus knew the entire Old Testament by heart. Historically there would have been other writings required for His memorization, so it may have included even more.

Jesus knew the Word to a level of mastery few will obtain but all of His followers can strive for. One thing is for sure: Jesus knew the Word.

> Whoever says he abides in him ought to walk in the same way in which he walked.
>
> —1 John 2:6

A Static Jedi knows the Word and commits it to memory. A Static Jedi journeys through the Word as the master did.

■ INTERNAL INQUIRY ■

1. How will you take the Word of God from head knowledge to heart knowledge—not so you keep it, but rather so that it keeps you?

2. How do you respond to learning Jesus knew that much of the Word?

3. Are you currently relying on Google or apps to give you knowledge but are ready to have it known within you?

■ EXTERNAL EXCHANGE ■

1. What is God speaking to you about memorizing His Word?

2. On a scale of one to ten, what is your current desire to know the Word of God?

3. Whatever your number may be, how can you better protect this desire you have?

Chapter 11

THE STATIC MASTER (PART 3): JESUS FASTED AND DISCIPLED

I WISH THERE WERE more places to discover and explore in the world today. You know, undiscovered, unexplored regions of the earth. Caves, forests, and lands. Perhaps a hidden lake. We have yet to go everywhere, but a good many places have seen the foot of man—and then the cameraman that follows him.

Explorers such as Magellan, Ferdinand de Soto, and Lewis and Clark, led by Sacagawea, had some exciting times. The chance to explore this planet by trekking to the unknown must have sparked that kindred adventure fire in them that dwells in me as well.

A Seasoned Explorer

When the North and South Poles had not yet experienced the foot of man (or his cameraman), an explorer named Richard E. Byrd ventured to them both.

On his second courageous expedition in 1934 to Antarctic, Byrd spent five of the most brutal winter months there alone, operating a meteorological station. All alone, surrounded by the one-act scene of frozen water, which would possibly become bottled water later, Byrd recorded in his field journal:

> I was learning…that a man can live profoundly without masses of things.[1]

It's true. We can live without many things we convince ourselves we need. Now hopefully we don't all have to take an expedition to the South Pole in complete solitude for five months to realize this list of "many things" we don't need. However, explore that list to the end, and you'll find there are a few items we really cannot live without. Shelter, love, and coffee would possibly be on that list. However, I'll admit the shelter of a coffee you love is not central to support life.

In truth, there are three things we can't live without:

- Air
- Water
- Food

Those three were present with Byrd during those five months. Without them he would have been present on a much shorter timeline.

Air. Water. Food.

We can never go without air, and we can never go without water. We never see weight-loss programs designed around breathing less. You'll never see a commercial about a new pill that helps you shed those unwanted pounds by replacing water with something else. We need both air and water to survive, period.

Food, however, dances to a different cadence.

We need food, but not in the amounts consumed by some people groups. (I would be living in one of those people groups. Likely, so are you.) Within all people, we find powerful biological wires sending signals to eat more food when we've had enough food. Even when our bodies have enough food, we are still attracted to more.

Overeating at Thanksgiving is a case in point. It's a national tradition.

The battle of willpower takes place when you see something you want to eat but know you don't need to eat it. If I could eat mac and cheese for every meal at Noodles & Company, for instance, and still be healthy for life, I would. With extra noodles and cheese. Because I don't want to go without. (You don't, either.)

Abstaining from your favorite food is a challenge, as it's not in our basic nature to forgo something we want. To pass it up. We like to eat, and we need to eat.

Without a struggle, there can be no progress.[2]
—**Fredrick Douglass**

But we also need to discover what Jesus knew and what Jesus practiced: going without food for a period of time to seek God instead.

To live as a seasoned explorer of the fast.

What is fasting? It may be a foreign thought to some—I know it was to me. Fasting is not on our horizon, as so many food stops litter the roads we travel.

While markets and fooderies existed in Jesus's time too, the concept and broad knowledge of fasting was arguably stronger then than it is now. Jesus lived in a time when fasting was an integrated, scheduled, and mandated part of the life of God's people.

In learning the Old Testament, Jesus would have memorized stories of fasts that had transpired. From His studies He would have understood the tree of the knowledge of good and evil, where staying away from food meant staying in connection with God. He would have known the additional fasting connections captured in the Tanakh—stories concerning Moses, David,

Elijah, Esther, Daniel, and Anna that all connect to fasting in some way. Jesus would have studied fasting in connection with deliverance from enemies in Judges, health in 2 Samuel, mourning in 1 Chronicles, forgiveness in Jonah, and danger and rescue in Esther.

Usually before a supernatural event in the Bible, the natural event of a fast occurred first. In Joel 2:28 we read:

> And it shall come to pass *afterward*, that I will pour out my Spirit on all flesh; your sons and your daughters shall prophesy, your old men shall dream dreams, and your young men shall see visions.
>
> —JOEL 2:28, EMPHASIS ADDED

Afterward?

After when?

After a conference?

After you finish the book?

Nope.

After a fast.

Jesus knew this, and so does a Static Jedi.

It was possibly no surprise to Jesus that when the Holy Spirit led Him into the wilderness, He was also led to fast for forty days. This was the prequel to launching His earthly ministry and ushering in a new supernatural happening. No miracle is recorded until after Jesus fasted, which begs a number of questions, one of which is: Would the result have been the same without His fasting? Many of the men whom God used in significant ways in the Old Testament spent time fasting in the desert too.

One absolute captured in the Gospels is that after Jesus fasted for forty days, the devil used food to try and deter what God was going to do. The devil is a schemer. If food worked to produce self-love in the garden, then food would work again to produce the same love that Jesus was going to die to redefine.

It is the same for us. The devil uses what worked in our past that Jesus died to redefine for our future. What the devil has used in the past in your life—the cycle of sin, the cycle of noise, the trap of all the static—he will use again, just as he did in the garden and then in the wilderness.

What changes this in the supernatural is nothing you have to do but what Jesus has already done. What changes in the flesh is fasting, and that is something we choose to do. It's something Jesus did. It's something a Static Jedi practices.

The noise can't stand the fast, though, for it allows us to stand above the noise.

 The devil uses what worked in our past that Jesus died to redefine for our future.
#staticjedi @ericsamueltimm

And so, without fasting in our lives, maybe the story ends differently.

With fasting, though, as we see in the story captured in Matthew, it ends for the devil in a failed attempt to overcome Jesus through temptation. Satan speaks to Jesus after He had not eaten for forty days. Turn this stone to bread, he says. Jesus responds with the Word that is locked in the chambers of His heart, not in the weak and fickle ways of Esau's stomach. Because Jesus knew the Word, He speaks, *"It is written, 'Man shall not live by bread alone, but by every word that comes from the mouth of God'"* (Matt. 4:4, emphasis added).

From the perspective of practice and privilege, Jesus fasted. He also would have fasted to follow the covenant and law as an obligation. A duty. Abstaining from food for spiritual purpose had already become a part of the culture before Jesus appeared on the scene. Specifically, in Hebrew culture, this practice of fasting would afflict the soul and was required by law as found in the Old Testament. This yearly scheduled removal of food to depend on God, to deny one's self, was a part of the even flow of calendar events back then. It was not a practice of "get to" as it is now.

The Day of Atonement, or Yom Kippur, was the tenth day of the seventh month. This calendar is specifically outlined in Leviticus and Numbers, and in Jesus's day, if you were a Jew, you honored Yom Kippur. Most still do. Honoring the holiday included fasting—the removal of food for spiritual purpose.

If you stop eating, you might assume you are afflicting only your body, for it is your body that needs to eat and needs fuel to function. However, the threads and functions of a fast run far deeper than that. The purpose is not so much to afflict the body as it is the breaking and humbling of the soul. Psalm 69:10 expresses it this way: *"When I wept and humbled my soul with fasting, it became my reproach"* (emphasis added). The focus was the inside rather than the outside. The inside always affects the outside.

Many heroes of the faith fasted. It's part of what it means to belong to the Order of They, remember? And in the landscape in which we now live, we have the same opportunity before us. Charles Spurgeon said, "Our seasons of fasting and prayer at the Tabernacle have been high days indeed; never has heaven's gate stood wider; never have our hearts been nearer to the central Glory."[3]

Jesus understood the connection between fasting and our souls, and He taught it. He taught fasting because He fasted to seek the Father over food.

The Static Master fasted.

A Static Jedi fasts.

And the Static Master is still fasting, waiting to drink from the fruit of the vine with us again.

> I tell you I will not drink again of this fruit of the vine until that day when I drink it new with you in my Father's kingdom.
>
> —MATTHEW 26:29

The Art of Creating Disciples

My son Xavier is a recorder. And the recording mechanism in his brain is always on. He watches my every move and repeats everything I teach him by way of firsthand education or subtle eavesdropping upon the happenings of my life. If you have kids, you know the feeling. Kids miss nothing. If you invest time in other people's kids, they are watching. Honor the parents and teach those kids well.

One New Year's celebration at our house, X-man—my son—was speaking in conversation to a child named Ravi. A massive end of the year bash was ensuing, and the decibel level in the house was continually on the rise. But through the celebration I overheard part of their interaction.

Both boys, around the age of three at the time, were sitting on the couch.

Ravi was wearing a Steelers sweatshirt—an uncommon shirt in the middle of rabid Vikings territory—and Xavier took direct notice of it. He then proceeded to interject his thoughts about Ravi's sweatshirt.

"Ravi," Xavier said. "I don't like Steelers. They're stupendous."

(*Stupendous* was the word locked in a neck-and-neck battle to replace the word *stupid* in Xavier's vocabulary, as X was recently bathed in the word *stupid* while watching the holiday classic *Charlie Brown Christmas*. Merry Christmas, Charlie Brown. Please thank Lucy for her concentrated effort to expand X's vocabulary.)

Ravi looked at Xavier and said, "I like the Steelers. They are awesome."

The conversation continued, with Xavier explaining further how he liked the Ravens and the Packers and Ravi further making a case for the Steelers and Vikings.

It occurred to me as I listened to this discussion that the boys had not engaged in the sport of football at an organized level of play. Further, they did not know the flow, rules, or basic concepts of the game. Neither of them had the slightest clue of the heated, long-seated rivalry between the Ravens/Steelers and the Vikings/Packers. So where did two three-year-old boys become so deeply convinced of their views of certain football teams?

Their dads.

As a die-hard Packers and Ravens fan, I was guilty. And I knew Shawn, Ravi's father, should also be questioned, for he was directly incriminated by the matching sweatshirt he wore that night, slightly larger than his son's. I certainly was guilty, for Xavier had been given a Packers sweatshirt and Ravens gear before he grasped the ability to walk. My son was becoming me because I was shaping him to my interests. I had made the choice. I wanted Xavier to follow me.

So it is with our Static Master. Jesus wants to make us like Him, just as a father would. This is why Jesus chooses us.

We find Jesus making such choices for people to follow Him in the Gospels. Growing up in Jesus's time was far different from the age Xavier is growing up in. The path back then did not include an elongated adolescence. Arguably in our age the loss of identity concerning what it means to be a man is found in this bright green light of adolescence. There is not a clear definition, a rite of passage, in much of the culture I live in. The question "When did you become a man?" is not easily answered. The same could be argued for the transition from a girl to a woman.

In Jesus's time, though, the path to becoming a man was defined and included following another man. Rabbis were the teachers, and beyond what would be similar to grade school, boys could continue their education with a rabbi of their choice. A boy would further train under a rabbi who would notice and choose him based on his ability to study and memorize the Torah. Upon finding the rabbi the boy wanted to emulate, he would approach the teacher after a required series of accomplishments and milestones had been completed.

Then he would learn the chosen rabbi's yoke. A yoke was the

way a rabbi interpreted the teachings of the Torah. Peering at the Torah through the perspective of a certain yoke was a way of looking at the teachings of God. When living out all teachings in the Torah, there would be this yoke spread throughout it, flavoring everything you did.

Like the yolk in scrambled eggs, the yoke of the rabbi would get everywhere and flavor everything.

Jesus had a yoke, and it was easy and light: "For my yoke is easy, and my burden is light" (Matt. 11:30). Here Jesus wasn't making reference to scrambled eggs or the yolk of an undeveloped chicken embryo. He was talking about a harness that would attach to oxen. Much like the heavy saddle a horse would wear, only more like a collar.

Jesus's yoke is found in two threads or commands in Mark:

> Jesus answered, "The most important is, 'Hear, O Israel: The Lord our God, the Lord is one. And you shall love the Lord your God with all your heart and with all your soul and with all your mind and with all your strength.'"
>
> —MARK 12:29–30

Jesus had a simple yoke: love God, and love your neighbor. However, let us not deceive ourselves into thinking that loving the Lord God with all our heart, soul, mind, and strength and loving our neighbor as ourselves comes easily, using the definitions of *love* and *neighbor* that Jesus gives. The definition of love found in 1 John 3:16 of laying down your life for someone else is easy to say and hard to live.

> By this we know love, that he laid down his life for us, and we ought to lay down our lives for the brothers.
>
> —1 JOHN 3:16

Maybe the yoke was easy in the sense that it was simple, but I know it's a challenge for me. It's a challenge for all of us. And it was a challenge for the disciples.

The students of Jesus, the disciples who followed Him, didn't choose Him as was the custom of the day. They didn't examine His yoke, hear of His teachings, or check the list of other options before declaring their choice. They didn't seek to follow Him or be chosen by Him. No, they became His disciples in a different way.

The rabbi chose them.

Jesus handpicked His inner circle and didn't wait for them to approach Him first. He sought them out. He went to them.

> Follow me, and I will make you fishers of men.
> —MATTHEW 4:19

> And Jesus said to them, "Follow me, and I will make you become fishers of men."
> —MARK 1:17

On the shore of the Sea of Galilee Jesus addressed His chosen few. "Follow Me," He said. "I choose you. You can be like Me." This is profound because rabbis didn't do this. Remember too this is before the miracles happened, before the crowds followed, and before the resurrection.

Have you ever wondered why they just left?

Even more incredulous is the men He selected. Fisherman. He chose fisherman! Like, one who fishes, with nets and stuff. To be a fisherman in the Hebrew landscape was to say you missed it. You didn't quite measure up. You didn't have what it took to become a teacher of the Torah and eventually work in the temple. So you were released to take up your family's trade. Sent back at a young age into the business of the family to labor for God the best you could. You weren't qualified for further discipleship. You were relegated to fish.

In Matthew 4:20 it seems strange that Peter and Andrew immediately left their nets and followed Jesus: *"Immediately they left their nets and followed him"* (emphasis added). Imagine a man walks up to you at work or school and says, "Quit your job, leave your life, and come, follow me." Talk about a Jerry Maguire moment! "Who's coming with me?"[4]

But Jesus, the master Torah teacher with authority, walked up to them and said, "Be who I am. You can be like Me. Even though you are fisherman and everyone else said that's all you will ever be, I see grand potential in you. I know you can be like Me—which is, in the lens of the landscape, way better than a fisherman. Here is your second chance."

This choosing illustrates Jesus's desire to make disciples.

And a Static Jedi makes disciples, just like the Static Master did.

It's a choice.

One that comes at a cost.

And it takes effort.

However, this is a choice a father would make. It is what the father desires.

> So Jesus said to them, "Truly, truly, I say to you, the Son can do nothing of his own accord, but only what he sees the Father doing. For whatever the Father does, that the Son does likewise."
>
> —JOHN 5:19

Duplication—the making of disciples—is the way of the Static Jedi. A Static Jedi ought to be found guilty when accused of doing it. Jesus certainly was guilty in His efforts toward duplication! And this is one more way we master the noise. Jesus had disciples and asks us to make them.

> Go therefore and make disciples of all nations, baptizing them in the name of the Father and of the Son and of the Holy Spirit, teaching them to observe all that I have commanded you. And behold, I am with you always, to the end of the age.
>
> —MATTHEW 28:19–20

The first step is making the choice. The Static Jedi decides to do it, just as the Static Master did before him. Then the Static Jedi creates disciples, just as the master...suggested? Asked nicely? Offered an opinion?

Commanded.

The Static Master rose early, withdrew for prayer, knew the Word, fasted, and chose and nurtured disciples. Go and do the same.

■ INTERNAL INQUIRY ■

1. What is standing in your way of choosing disciples or fasting?

2. How are you replicating Christ and reproducing Him?

3. What will your fast look like? What will you be seeking of God through this time?

■ EXTERNAL EXCHANGE ■

1. Who do you feel like God is calling you to reproduce yourself into? To disciple?

2. Why is fasting a "get to" not a "have to"?

3. How can our church seek bread from heaven more than bread from earth?

Chapter 12

NEW BEGINNING

I'LL BE HONEST. I like when people take me out to eat and then they pay. (This is not a ploy for the next time you see me to take me to a restaurant. But seriously, you can. We'll have great conversation over good food.) In all seriousness, buying a meal and sharing an experience is a simple kindness I enjoy.

When was the last time you paid for someone's meal? When you were planning on doing it, did you wait until the end of the meal, when the check came, to tell them, "I got this. No, really—put away your money."

You know you did.

I sure do!

If you let that gem out of your mouth before everyone orders, it's open season on the menu of "why not both?" Your guests then order all kinds of costly bubbly drinks, appetizers, and extra shrimp, followed by the flaming almond blonde brownie ice cream chocolate wedge cheesecake pie with that sexy mint leaf placed upon the dab of whipped heaven. (There's never enough whipped cream. I want to dig through the blizzard of whipped goodness on a sugar expedition to find the treasured pie that waits beneath. Whipped cream marks the spot.)

As I said, I like free food. When my meal is paid for me, I eat and enjoy at no cost to myself.

But it costs someone something.

It costs me often too in reality, because I'm part of what officially unofficial sociologists like to call "the sandwich generation." My dad and I go to Subway, and I do my best to buy my dad's sandwich. When my sons are hungry, I pay for their subs. When I'm purchasing lunch for my father or sons, it costs me something.

The "sandwich generation."

Some of you know the feeling.

It costs.

Lunch will always cost someone something.

There is no free lunch.

And walls don't come down for free, either.

Walls Are Expensive

God doesn't like barriers. We don't like the cost to remove them. But the walls must come down. The noise must be mastered. And Jesus, the Static Master, gives us five keys to do it.

We'll cover the five keys in depth in the chapters ahead, but let me first stress the importance of integrating these keys into your life. They are foundational. They'll help you through the process of understanding God as a person who has no grandchildren. With the proper investment of time, no matter your past, investing time into these five keys that Jesus lived and taught will help the Static Jedi master the noise.

When we are slaves to the noise, it creates fortifications inside us that keep us from entering the city—the new realm where the Static Jedi thrives.

The realm where the Static Master lived.

But on the other side of that wall is a richer, fuller life with God. The thief comes to steal and destroy, but Christ came to give you life and life more abundant. I personally don't look for a demonic force behind every single object, but ask yourself: Is it possible the thief is stealing our time, our abundant life, one box at a time, as illustrated in chapter 1?

We can reclaim our time and peace.

Become a master of the static—a Static Jedi.

Occasionally the task may seem impossible, but not for God. Through Him we are able to accomplish the impossible. Our flesh can die. After all, it's only flesh. Time can be captured. After all, we can invest in a better net.

We just have to do our part in the process.

When Jericho Crumbled

Joshua had to do his part too. God promised the Hebrews a land that was rich and able to sustain them. One huge problem: Jericho was surrounded by immense walls.

God decided to tear down these walls a little differently than the norm. He didn't have them use huge catapults, fire, or a massive battering ram the likes of which you'd see on *Braveheart* or the Lord of the Rings trilogy.

God decided, for the tearing down of this wall, He would use silence.

It always seems impossible until it's done.[1]

—Nelson Mandela

To carry out this wall-breaking silence, two specific types of fruit had to be present in Joshua's life: obedience and discipline. This fruit grows strong with the two stones and five keys we're covering in this book—and without them, Joshua would have had to change the battle plan.

Yes, obedience and discipline were growing on the tree of Joshua's life. And like lone oaks standing in fields of mediocrity, those who produce these fruits as Joshua did will endure. These trees prevail when the setting sinks.

This must be clear to any Static Jedi. To respond the way God desires, rather than react the way we want, God tells us to stand when all else deteriorates.

Even when it's noisy,
it seems impossible,
the setting isn't trendy,
the math doesn't add up,
and it goes against logical explanation.

God sometimes defies our version of logic, don't you think? That's what He did for Joshua. He instructed Joshua to put the priests and the ark of the covenant at the front of the army—oh yeah, and to assemble everyone in silence. Without speaking, the people walked around the huge barriers toward the life God had for His people.

> You shall march around the city, all the men of war going around the city once. Thus shall you do for six days. Seven priests shall bear seven trumpets of rams' horns before the ark. On the seventh day you shall march around the city seven times, and the priests shall blow the trumpets. And when they make a long blast with the ram's horn, when you hear the sound of the trumpet, then all the people shall shout with a great shout, and the wall of the city will fall down flat, and the people shall go up, everyone straight before him.
> —JOSHUA 6:3–5

Trusting, Joshua did as he was told. He put to death all the excuses, waded through the waters of doubt, and walked in obedience and discipline. And on the seventh day the praise rose to the heavens.

And the walls came tumbling down.

Your wall can fall. A breakthrough happened then, and a breakthrough will happen now. Your walls of stone built with the mortar of noise will tumble, and you can enter into the rich and full life God prepared for you.

I believe it is God's heart to know us deeply and intimately so that our walls crumble and we enter into a fuller, more Spirit-filled life, standing secure on knowledge and truth rather than precariously tiptoeing on mere information. Entering this city of righteousness—not self-righteousness—means building on obedience and discipline. It means standing on the two stones with the five keys in hand and at work in our lives.

In this place love freely flows.

Love is the power of the Static Jedi.

It's what the world needs.

The Bad News Never Ends

Becoming like the Static Master is a never-ending process— that's the bad news. But just let the bad news never end. In the next seven days we're going to stand on the two stones and pursue the five keys, but these practices must continue influencing the rest of our days on this earth. The process of mastery is the goal, but even on our best day our righteousness, compared to the righteousness of God, is still like filthy rags. Like a nasty cold washcloth in the bottom of the kitchen sink saturated with food chunks, egg yolks, and chicken juice.

Nasty.

Here is the good news. In our quest for the mastery of noise, we become more like Jesus. The whole point of Christianity is to become His disciple, to live how He would have us live, and to love how He showed us to love, creating more disciples in the process.

By seeking the goal to become like Jesus, we accomplish this goal along the way and not by way of the end. The journey is the first destination.

Buckle Up—Impact Is Imminent

In the next chapter I'm going to ask you do something hard, something I wish someone would have asked me to do long ago. So buckle up—impact is imminent. It's total, complete, utter, absolute, and thorough. It will require some action and responsibility on your part.

The tasks ahead are not easy and may require premeditated

organizational agility. In this digitally connected age and the accompanying responsibilities we have at work and home, you may have to prepare for the challenges. You may have to get up early or try something you haven't done before. You might have to seek counsel or more information in the pages of this book to greater expound on the tasks ahead. You may find the daily tasks rooted in noise must be addressed and possibly modified. You might have to put in place alternative plans based on your calling, not based on the noise. You might need to make advance phone calls, unplug your devices, and write a final status update.

Action springs not from thought but a readiness for responsibility.[2]

—Dietrich Bonhoeffer

In fact, let's do that now.

I challenge you to post this one statement on your Facebook, Twitter, and maybe draw a sign and take a picture of it for your Instagram account. For the next seven days also use it as your e-mail auto-responder if possible. Leave it up for the next few days while you begin mastering the noise in this Static Jedi training.

Post, Tweet, pic and auto-respond one last time the following:

Becoming a Static Jedi. #staticjedi @ericsamueltimm

Why? So I can sell more books? Please don't read that into my intention here. If more books are purchased and read, so be it. I never took an art class past high school, and I got Cs and Ds in English classes. I didn't sign up for this. The next speaking event doesn't motivate me, nor does obtaining followers or checks. I would be content to stay home pruning my bonsai trees and working in my garden, walking the road with my community each day. Instead, I'm compelled to offer these written pages to you like a canvas, creating art by obedience to the Word of

God, a love-like fire shut up in my bones. Thus, my bonsai trees died long ago and the garden is usually no more than a beautiful patch of fruitful, untilled soil.

Heart on the Table

My intention is to spark conversations between you and the ones in your circle of influence. Then it's to turn that spark into a blaze of fire that burns deeply into the people surrounding your life. People you touch directly with your time. I want to encourage you to grow by digging deep into Scripture and then challenge you to share your discoveries so others may be encouraged and challenged by you, not me.

You will look more like Jesus as you radically invest your time differently. That flesh that holds you like a puppet now will have its strings ripped from its sockets through the process of fasting. The aim is to create churches full of disciples, not just Christians—disciples without walls who have committed to memory whole books, not just verses, of God's Word.

 I want to see us rising above fast and easy microwave Christianity with a decompartmentalized, committed life that makes Jesus a part of every moment.
#staticjedi @ericsamueltimm

Do you hear me screaming with tattered lungs here? My prayer for us all of us is that we would love and genuinely know our God and then know and genuinely love our neighbors. I long to see a movement of Christ followers with depth, true sensitivity, and reliance on His Spirit, followers of Jesus waking before the rest of their world wakes up in order to seek God for their world in prayer. Disciples standing above the noise on the two stones integrated into our foundation.

I want to see us rising above fast and easy microwave Christianity with a decompartmentalized, committed life that makes Jesus a part of every moment.

It is worth the effort.

I hope for each of us to have a complex and simple understanding of the complex and simple God we serve. May we know and move in His will and die to our flesh.

This is my cry, so shall it be your cry.

Let us echo the sound,

the sound of chains breaking.

No longer chained to the noise, we seek the vine.

The vine makes the fruit, not us—

A process unfolding with no one but Jesus looking,

For no other reward than what is seen by the Father.

Let this be what we seek.

Become disciples of the Static Master Jesus.

And then produce disciples, as He told us to.

Now draw lines in the sand and choose where you stand.

People respect when you choose a side.

They question when you straddle.

He was with the woman at the well

On the other side of the line.

It doesn't matter—your past.

Change the future. Cross the line.

Not lukewarm. Be hot or cold.

I choose to burn

For the rest of my life.

Move toward mastery with Jesus as the Master.

Stand on new ground that exists behind the wall.

Are you ready?

It will cost you something.

There is no free lunch.

■ INTERNAL INQUIRY ■

1. Does your heart echo this cry?

2. What is the most difficult thing about this next step?

3. What is the hardest noise for you to escape?

4. Are you ready to pursue God though it may cost more than you anticipate?

■ EXTERNAL EXCHANGE ■

1. How can we help one another prepare for the start?

2. What ways is God calling you to forge ahead and trust more in Him?

3. What is the cry inside your heart for your life, children, church, city, and world?

Chapter 13

GREEN MEN SPEAK TRUTH

B EFORE JOSHUA ARRIVED at Jericho, only to march around
the protective walls in silence for seven days on his way to
victory, God's people had to cross the Jordan River. Part of this
crossing began long before the Israelites reached the far shore.
Read it with me:

> Then Joshua rose early in the morning and they set out
> from Shittim. And they came to the Jordan, he and all
> the people of Israel, and lodged there before they passed
> over. At the end of three days the officers went through the
> camp and commanded the people, "As soon as you see the
> ark of the covenant of the LORD your God being carried
> by the Levitical priests, then you shall set out from your
> place and follow it. Yet there shall be a distance between
> you and it, about 2,000 cubits in length. Do not come near
> it, in order that you may know the way you shall go, for
> you have not passed this way before." Then Joshua said to
> the people, "Consecrate yourselves, for tomorrow the LORD
> will do wonders among you."
>
> —JOSHUA 3:1–5

In my Bible I highlighted verses 3 and 4: "As soon as you
see the ark...then you shall set out from your place and follow
it" and "You may know the way you shall go, for you have not
passed this way before." For mastery of the static to become a

reality, you must move from your current position and strategy to follow Jesus. You will know the way to go because Jesus will lead the way. Even though you have not lived this way before, you will know the way because you are following the way.

In verse 5 Joshua gives further instructions to the people: "Consecrate yourselves, for tomorrow the LORD will do wonders among you." Joshua is asking everyone to consecrate themselves as the law at that time commanded. This law would include many ritual cleansings, many specified garments, and a list of boxes to check before it was complete. Thank You, Jesus, for not destroying the law but for checking off the check boxes for us!

> Do not think that I have come to abolish the Law or the Prophets; I have not come to abolish them but to fulfill them.
> —MATTHEW 5:17

That word *consecrate* in Joshua 3 is *qadash*. It means "to say, to prepare, dedicate, set apart in preparation to watch God do amazing things."[1] This concept of consecration means, then, to set apart for a period of time, to give the consecrated event a start and an end. For example, consecrating a day means that once that day passes, the following days return to the normal routine.

There Is a Choice

A Static Jedi lives consecrated not for a scheduled event that is confined by a beginning and an end, but rather consecrates himself to eternally seek Jesus. Consecration to Jesus, not the noise, is the way of the Static Jedi.

To live concentrated, we must live consecrated.

Let's start as Joshua did before Jericho: dedicating time to the special purpose of seeking the sacred. Especially because the majority of our time is desecrated in purposeless investment. From this hurried life, we build walls because we invest our time in the wrong things. However, change is possible no matter what the past. Whether you come from oil or water, you must choose change.

 To live concentrated, we must live consecrated. #staticjedi @ericsamueltimm

---

The foundation for this quest is the undergirding pursuit of the person of Jesus. This focus sets the stage for us to launch. Pitfalls may lie ahead in this journey, and false masters will rise, but through the example of Jesus, the Static Master, we can embark on the journey to master the noise. I haven't always lived here, in the quest to master the noise and to become a Static Jedi. It's a commitment I've since made—to live as Jesus asks me to.

We can make progress.

In full-time ministry, as I described in chapter 1 of this book, caught in the perpetual undertow of the noise, choice for consecration is where my journey began. I wanted to emulate how Jesus lived.

I want you to emulate Him too.

Seven-Day Challenge

For the next seven days I'm asking you to set a goal that I assure you can be accomplished but will look different for each of us. Maybe it's not just you but a group of people with you or your entire church who journeys together through this.

The goal is to live completely free of your noise.

To start, become free of all digital communication and interaction for seven days.

Seven days of silence.

Just like you can't use your cell phone during takeoff on an airplane, you can't use it for the next seven days. No screens, no Internet, no phone—nothing that runs on a battery or begins with the letter *i*.

Some of you are already chomping at the bit. Those of you in the daily workforce or who have loved ones living abroad or sons in the military or other special circumstances will find this an additionally poignant challenge. Others of you are going to easily accomplish this.

It's a tough commitment to remove the technological noise when our lives rely heavily on that noise, including e-mail, phones, and LED screens. You will have to adjust accordingly. Removing these things from our lives means the noise can no longer have a foothold.

For some this might be impossible. That's OK. There is no pass or fail on this consecration exercise. Jesus already passed, and if you are in Jesus, you passed.

Now pursue.

Don't wait for a seven-day vacation run or the perfect time to do it, like when you go camping or live in a hole. Merely do your best and start somewhere. There is never an easy way or time to do this. Change is usually hard. Maybe for you, it's just shutting off the TV, staying off the computer, or remaining absent from social media sites. For me it meant combining all those things and more.

However, I encourage you to preplan the removal of the noise as much as possible to set yourself up for success. Whatever you put into this, you will get out. It's up to you. Investing time with Jesus always pays a high return. He always gives more than we put in. You can't out give Jesus.

In addition to the removal of digital noise, shield yourself from analog noise. I suggest a fast from reading the printed newspaper, magazines, or other publications. The only book you'll read during this time is the Bible and my book.

Kidding!

Just the Bible.

My small group's favorite board games Ticket to Ride and

Carcassonne are on my list to remove from my life for these seven days too.

Seek silence.

Reject the noise.

We need to find God, and he cannot be found in
noise and restlessness. God is the friend of silence.
See how nature—trees, flowers, grass—grow in
silence; see the stars, the moon and sun, how they
move in silence.... The more we receive in silent
prayer, the more we can give in our active life. We
need silence to be able to touch souls. The essential
thing is not what we say, but what God says to
us and through us. All our words will be useless
unless they come from within—words which do
not give the light of Christ increase the darkness.[2]

—Mother Teresa

Consecrate these seven days to spend as much time as possible in alone time with Jesus, balancing it with real time spent with your family and community.

How weird will it be when you're hanging out with your friends and you are actually present and accounted for? Refreshing. You'll be engaged rather than distracted. No longer staring at a screen, lost in some other conversation.

Live Differently

Begin to destroy the walls with this radical shift toward consecration for seven days. What are you going to do during those handful of days? How will you fill the vacuum created by the elimination of digital demands on your time?

Good question.

You are going to take hold of the keys.

You must live by the five keys that a Static Jedi wields—keys Jesus showed us through His humble example. Without these keys it's difficult to live a life of clarity unlocked from the cycle of noise that silently shackles us all.

I want to present these keys as elements integrated into the seven days of this consecration period and then incorporated far past the seven days, into our everyday lives. But I caution you that possessing these keys will require you to do additional digging on your own. They did for me. Along the way I will suggest resources I found in my own quest to become like the Static Master, as challenging you without equipping you would bring defeat. So dress in your armor for the battle, and I will serve as a guide and Jesus will serve as the map. In other writings I'm currently penning and plan to publish, I will explore these things more personally, but until then I will point you to other works. Most importantly I will do my best to point toward Jesus.

Further, I will intentionally start where I started in each journey not from a perspective of haughty mastery but to offer my personal experience. I have not arrived, but I certainly have decided to leave.

You too have to decide to embark on the first step.

You have to choose.

To quote Yoda for the first time in this book, "Do or do not. There is no try."

It's your choice.

Turn the page, and read on about what to do.

Or close the book to not continue.

Pray with me what I penned to start my own journey first:

Creator of this universe, even my small, drowning heart.

I'm sinking and I need a rescue for my heavy, noisy heart.

"Hear my cry and save me," I scream with deepest plea.

To You, and You alone, I speak such words, I decree.

My life is noisy, past is broken, as You already know.

I'm withered, I'm guilty, but longing to be seen as snow.

Jesus, Your name I speak, I ask and seek, for I'm drowning, sinking

and cannot save what I did not make. There is no other my soul to take.

So replace my heart, rescue my life, work in me, remake my art.

You alone have the power to mend a sinner, a wretch, a slave from sin.

From this noisy heart, with my last old breath, I call to You, believing in Your death.

Declaring Your blood was shed for me and Your scars enough, this I now see.

I need not new ones, I need only trust,

In Your unfailing rescue,

For You rose from death and dust.

Jesus, even my small, noisy heart,

I place in Your hands, I capture a new start.

Help me. Jesus, I confess with my mouth without fear, with hope

And without any doubt.

■ INTERNAL INQUIRY ■

1. How have you lived diluted?

2. What are you hoping to see in your life from your seven-day consecration?

3. What's standing in your way to carry out the challenge to completely sever the ties between you and the noise for a period of time?

■ EXTERNAL EXCHANGE ■

1. What's the difference between biblical consecration and fasting?

2. How can we live differently?

3. Will you take the Static Jedi challenge?

4. Break down the statement, "Whatever you put into it, you get out of it." Do you believe this is true in our everyday lives?

Chapter 14

EARLY ARTS OF DRAWING AND PRAYER

JESUS DEMONSTRATED THE necessary keys to discipleship in His own life. He daily consecrated His seconds, minutes, and hours from the moment He awoke. Let's look at the five keys the Static Master holds and hands to us.

KEY #1: Rise Early

As I shared earlier in this book, many past followers of Christ were known for their early mornings. Slow down—pump the breaks. I'm not asking you to get up at 3:30 a.m. or to rise to Martin Luther status by getting up four hours early every morning to pray and study.

However, let's begin somewhere. We may be *willing* to set the alarm three hours earlier, but our flesh is weak. Jesus understood this.

> And he came and found them sleeping, and he said to Peter, "Simon, are you asleep? Could you not watch one hour? Watch and pray that you may not enter into temptation. The spirit indeed is willing, but the flesh is weak." And again he went away and prayed, saying the same words. And again he came and found them sleeping, for their eyes were very heavy, and they did not know what to answer him.
>
> —MARK 14:37–40

Did you catch that last line? "And they did not know what to answer Him."

I can just see it. "Hmm, Jesus. It's like this. We were, um, well, OK, seriously, um, I was thinking, well, you and my dad said once…OK, so can I start over?"

I want to know what to say. Maybe, "I was sleeping. I'm tired, but I'm working on it"?

Our flesh may be weak, but it can be trained to be strong. Just watch the Olympics. Lots of strong flesh there that I'm sure had to be trained to wake early in the morning to begin those hard and daily practices.

As a man Jesus disciplined Himself to rise early. In the Gospels it was recorded multiple times—and it should be recorded in the stories of our lives too.

So for the next seven days I am asking you to get up fifteen minutes earlier than your normal routine would dictate. Introduce freedom into your morning. And peace. Start small so you see big results. Little decisions over time make a big impact on our lives. Having fifteen minutes of consecrated time in the morning is a great first step.

For the twenty-one days following those first seven days, set your alarm an additional fifteen minutes earlier each week until you get to a place where you possess sixty additional minutes daily.

Where shall the world be found, where will the word resound? Not here, there is not enough silence.[1]

—T. S. Eliot

I know it's initially difficult to get up in the morning, but remind yourself that anything good comes at a cost. Start the gradual change. A book that helped me personally inspect my cycle of life and adjust accordingly was *The Power of Habit* by Charles Duhigg. Maybe it will help you too.

The goal by the end of thirty days is to be getting up one hour before everything else begins. Before the rush. Before the hurry. Beyond sixty minutes where you stop is up to you. I experience my best times with God when I'm up one or more hours before the first event, scheduled appointment, workout, or the rest of my family.

To accomplish this, I have had to responsibly invest my time the night before. Most problems in the morning can be solved the night before. What are the habits that drive you? Take an inventory of the events of the night preceding the morning to better equip the morning for focus. Having trouble sleeping? Studies show that people sleep better when all digital viewing is removed one to three hours before retiring. Digital devices stimulate the brain, and just before bed is when you want to be slowing down, preparing for deep rest. Board games and reading are activities that slow the brain for sleep.

The early morning Static Jedi is then prepared for the next key.

KEY #2: Withdraw to Draw Toward God

Get some paper. Write on it the word *listen*. How do we accomplish the task of listening? We focus with our ears and attention. We process the silence, body language, or words spoken. It's a process that involves us actively being silent. If you try and listen to someone while you are moving or talking, the task is challenging. It's frustrating for the one speaking to you too. The absence of silence muddies the message.

To listen more clearly, simply rearrange the investment of time. The key to listening is found within the word itself. Use the letters found in the word *listen* and rearrange them to spell another word: *silent*. Write that word too on your paper. From this rearrangement of time, seeking silence, we become better listeners when Jesus speaks.

Early mornings embody silence.

Peace.

Before feeding the crowds, Jesus asks His disciples to do something simple and profound: to withdraw to a quiet place of peace.

> And he said to them, "Come away by yourselves to a desolate place and rest a while." For many were coming and going, and they had no leisure even to eat. And they went away in the boat to a desolate place by themselves. Now many saw them going and recognized them, and they ran there on foot from all the towns and got there ahead of them. When he went ashore he saw a great crowd, and he had compassion on them, because they were like sheep without a shepherd. And he began to teach them many things.
>
> —Mark 6:31–34

Then the feeding of the five thousand took place with that abundance of fish and bread. There were even leftovers! What if Jesus hadn't rested? Would that miracle have taken place? If Jesus had to rest and also asked His disciples to rest, why would we be excluded from finding a quiet place to be still and pray?

If we slow the pace of life, our lives seem to pace with life; keeping time like a distant runner bound for gold.

—Eric Samuel Timm

How many moments find us unprepared because we did not first seek the solitude of a quiet place? How many people could we feed because we first took time to feed ourselves? Jesus is asking each of us to come by ourselves with Him to a quiet place and receive rest. From this place of stillness we feed more people than we could do in our own strength. We receive strength flowing from Him. In stillness.

> Be still, and know that I am God.
>
> —Psalm 46:10

The noise hides the stillness.
Awake earlier and find it.

For the next seven days find a quiet spot each morning and go there. Show up.

This place, sometimes referred as a closet, or the wilderness, is the quiet place found in Scripture: "He makes me lie down in green pastures. He leads me beside still waters" (Ps. 23:2). I want you to go every day to the same location to seek God in the morning. It could be the woods, a secluded area of a park, or an actual closet. There should be no other people around you. I find my preference is a place in nature.

For seven days withdraw from people to draw near to God. Once a year plan a one- to three-day hunting, camping, sight-seeing, backpacking, or fishing trip to withdraw from people for an extended period.

I have enjoyed discovering a practice common in Catholic communities as well as many Protestant churches known as the silent retreat. This is usually a three-day period where there is no conversation but the one you have with the Father. It's still practiced by our brothers and sisters in Catholic communities; they have become masters of the facilitation of this kind of retreat. You can find information on retreat centers near you online at jesuit.org. Or better yet, just walk into a Catholic church and have a conversation with a person face-to-face.

During such escapes, no matter the method, one constant should be present: prayer. When we empty our lives of people, conversation, and other distractions to create space for conversation with God, prayer is critical to this daily time of withdrawing.

There are wrong ways to pray and right ways to pray. Jesus explains that we are not to pray as the hypocrites. I used to think prayer involved me doing most of the speaking. OK, maybe *all* the talking! It was up to me to fill the silence. I've since learned that prayer contains parts listening and parts speaking. Prayer is a two-way conversation between me and God.

In his book *A Better Way to Pray* Pastor Andrew Wommack asks, "What would be left of most Christians' prayer lives if all the repenting for sin, asking for things, and intercession were subtracted? Hardly anything." Wommack goes on to show that while Adam and Eve, before the Fall, had no sin, no lack, no need to contend with evil, they still "prayed—communed with God—every single day!"[2]

 There are wrong ways to pray and right ways to pray. Jesus explains that we are not to pray as the hypocrites.
#staticjedi @ericsamueltimm

To commune with the Father in prayer, not just in the time we plan to pray in the morning but throughout the rest of the day, how is this tangibly lived out? A. W. Tozer's *Attributes of God* reeks with this decompartmentalized life as we start seeking, praising, and praying more to God. Once you learn and discover more of God's attributes, you realize things about this process you may not have noticed before. Chapters expounding on this practical application are also found in *Celebration of Discipline*. In this classic by Richard Foster, the writer illustrates, "Whether alone or among people, we always carry with us a portable sanctuary of the heart."[3]

On paper you could call your portable sanctuary of the heart written prayers, your prayer log, or a prayer journal. Pastor Andy (the one with the coffee beans) and I call them prayer cards. I have started to carry these prayer cards with me. Five little index cards labeled *praise*, *plans*, *provision*, *people*, and *perspective*. Like old-school math flashcards, they remind me of a key to the formula for a life in mastery of the noise: prayer.

The index cards are labeled as such because of Jesus's teachings on how to pray in the Lord's Prayer (Matt. 6:9–13). Read it with me below. I will put my comments below the words of Jesus's prayer to show where each card flows. I'm not establishing doctrine here, and you don't have to use prayer cards, but if your prayer life seems not to be working, consider inspecting your prayers. I have found it's not often God who needs the refocusing or fixing. Pretty much every time it's me.

Pray, then, like this:

> Our Father in heaven, hallowed be your name.

Praise. Offer praise for who He is—not what you want, just who He is.

> Your kingdom come, your will be done, on earth as it is in heaven.

Plans. Commit your plans to be His plans. His plans be done in your life! Invite the kingdom of God to settle upon your praise and your plans.

> Give us this day our daily bread.

Provision. Seek provision for your daily needs. What you need each day, ask God to give it to you.

> And forgive us our debts, as we also have forgiven our debtors.

People. Give thanks by requesting a person's forgiveness for my wrongs and asking for the grace to forgive other people.

> And lead us not into temptation, but deliver us from evil.

People. Ask for God to keep you on the right path and to provide a way out when evil seeks to keep you hostage.

And that's where it ends.

Or does it? Some translations continue to add the phrase *"[For Yours is the kingdom and the power and the glory forever. Amen.]"* There are these little brackets [ ] around the words.

Why is that?

While it is certainly not a wrong statement from a theological perspective, 1 Chronicles echoes this phrase reworded:

> Yours, O LORD, is the greatness and the power and the glory and the victory and the majesty, for all that is in the heavens and in the earth is yours. Yours is the kingdom, O LORD, and you are exalted as head above all.
>
> —1 CHRONICLES 29:11

Why is the line in some Bibles and not in others?

The addition of the ending to the Lord's Prayer is a source of debate among Bible scholars because its being or not being in the Bible is not totally certain. I don't want to delve into the abyss of manuscript study here, for we may never return! However, the New Testament you hold in your hands is based upon two different classes, or families, of manuscripts: Alexandrian and Byzantine. Most of the time the two classes or families of text agree. Yet they do have differences. The New Testament left in a hotel drawer is the King James translation, and it is Byzantine. Otherwise it's mostly the Alexandrian.

So why is it is some Bibles and not in others?

Long story short: Because man can screw up.

Which leads me to the last prayer card: perspective.

> [For Yours is the kingdom and the power and the glory forever. Amen.]

Perspective. Ask God to help you to have the perspective that although man may try and get it right, apart from Him we get it wrong. Tell God, "I want Your perspective in my praise, my plans, my provision, and the people around me. Your kingdom, Your glory, and Your power! Nothing I can manufacture. Let me see beyond the boxes I put You in. You are not to be in a [ ]."

Why prayer cards? For me, remembering everything I need to is a challenge. If it's not on the list when I go to the grocery store, it's not coming home. I'll forget. These cards help me remember what I'm praying for. I also like to find scriptures in God's Word that pertain to the cards and write those scriptures out on the card for deeper memorization. A few of my community members at my church pray scriptures mined from the treasure of the Word over each heading on their cards and have seen God move through prayer.

It may be somewhat different for you. What is the same for us all, though, is that God answers prayer. And when God does answer our prayers, what's our response? Or when our prayers aren't instantly answered, what's our response? Usually doubt. When I cross that prayer off the list, God answered and I'm not going to forget. If the devil tries to remind you of what God didn't do, it's nice to have some evidence that says otherwise.

On your way to master the static, your prayers travel with you, just as Jesus is your constant companion. Acknowledge this. Be aware and looking for the presence of Christ, and you will see it. "Pray without ceasing" (1 Thess. 5:17). And if you think it will help you stay focused in prayer, bring your prayer cards. Or just go with the antithesis of focused prayer: the shotgun approach.

I've found in the stillness of prayer, in early morning times, when I'm withdrawing from people, that God speaks loud to me. When I listen, God speaks during prayer and declares truth in His Word. A Static Jedi studies, wrestles with, and discovers His Word.

And memorizes the declarations.

■ INTERNAL INQUIRY ■

1. Who are you trying to be like? Do your actions, habits, and character match?

2. Are you waking up early to be with Jesus?

3. What might you be missing by not being with Jesus in the silence of the morning?

4. What would you put on your prayer cards? Why not start?

■ EXTERNAL EXCHANGE ■

1. What benefits come from withdrawing from the noise and crowds?

2. What time are you going to set your alarm for to spend time with Jesus?

3. Where are some places you connect best with God?

4. Why do you think God made the wilderness?

Chapter 15

SWORDS IN HOTEL DRAWERS

Let's turn now to the third key Christ gives us—knowing His Word.

KEY #3: Knowing God's Word

If you don't have a Bible, stay at a hotel. You'll find one in the drawer. Take it out, turn to the opening page, and cross out "placed by" and insert "taken by." Then change "Gideons" to your name. Use a gold or silver pen from someone's scrapbooking drawer and write in cursive. Because cursive is fancier and found on most customized Bibles.

Kidding.

Don't do that.

Buy a Bible from my publisher. Wink, wink.

The truth regarding most things in life is that you don't need look any further than a hotel drawer for the answers to the challenge for change: God's Word. The Bible in that hotel drawer has completed a monumental journey to arrive at that location, and when we pick it up, the journey begins again.

We must study the Word.

May this be the genesis of a willingness in your heart. First John 2:6 says, "Whoever says he abides in him ought to walk in the same way in which he walked." Jesus, our Static Master, knew the Word—He had the Word memorized by heart, and so we as Static Jedis will strive to do the same.

It's mind-boggling to think that Jesus and rabbis of His time memorized the entire Old Testament! One of my favorite earthly sources for understanding the landscape through the Jewish viewpoint is Ray Vander Laan. I hope to meet him one day. His life is dedicated to helping you and me understand the Christianity of the West through the lens of the East, where the stories in the Bible took place.

One other is James Emery White. I hope to meet him again someday as well. Illuminating the historical mind-set that is in stark contrast to today, White's work calls for the importance of a mind for God in the midst of the serious times in which we live.

> The great opposition to reading is what I allow to fill my time instead of reading. To say we have no time to read is not really true; we simply have chosen to use our time for other things, or have allowed our time to be filled to the exclusion of reading. So don't add reading to your to-do list. Just stop doing the things that keep you from doing it. But read.[1]
>
> —James Emery White

To memorize seven hundred thousand-plus words, depending on the translation, provided you live seventy years and begin at age six, you would commit to memory approximately:

10,937 words each year
210 words each week
30 words per day
every day for 64 years.

With that schedule, you would have it down in over six decades.

Provided you remembered the previous day's thirty words for the sixty-four years.

Pump the breaks. However, let's start somewhere.

If Jesus read and reread the Torah time and again until He memorized it, I would offer a thought. As Christians we should read and reread the Gospels that are about the one we follow. *Christian* means "one who follows Christ."

It's not an adjective, meaning it doesn't describe something. The word is a noun, and from this perspective we must be noun Christians not adjective Christians. We are to be deeply motivated by the love of verbs—reaching, loving, serving, forgiving, knowing, and following, to name a few. We must know the Word as the master Jesus did and follow Him through the study of it.

For the next seven days read the Gospel of Matthew. Do not read it to simply get through it. Read the Book so it gets through you. Let it sink into your heart and inspect your actions. Or if you would like a more aggressive track, read all four Gospels in those seven days.

Whatever your choice, read the Scripture on printed paper. An actual hold-in-your-hands Bible. Old-school style. If you read it on your phone, your phone can ring, texts come in, and games are just a click away—not to mention you would be breaking the seven-day challenge altogether.

Journey with pen and journal in hand. All books are best explored, in my opinion, when the pages are paper and we hold a pen in our hand with something to write upon. This will allow you to write and ask questions when needed.

Read the Word with the intention to be changed by it, not to change the pages.

Consume God's Word not to get through it but so it comes through you.

Put on your SPECS—read God's Word by keeping in mind the following:

- ❀ Sins to confess and repent

- ❀ Promises to claim

- ❀ Examples to follow or not follow

- ❀ Commands to obey

- ❀ Significant truths or statements not yet understood

Looking though these SPECS is helpful, for they help apply the truth found in the pages of our lives. This approach to Scripture has been broadly taught and is one I personally like.

Here's what a seven-day reading plan looks like for the Gospel of Matthew:

1. Day 1: Matthew 1–5

2. Day 2: Matthew 6–10

3. Day 3: Matthew 11–13

4. Day 4: Matthew 14–17

5. Day 5: Matthew 18–21

6. Day 6: Matthew 22–25

7. Day 7: Matthew 26–28

Or if you want to be more aggressive, here is what the seven-day reading plan looks like for all four Gospels:

1. Day 1: Matthew 1–15

2. Day 2: Matthew 16–28

3. Day 3: Mark 1–13

4. Day 4: Mark 14–Luke 8

5. Day 5: Luke 9–20

6. Day 6: Luke 21–John 7

7. Day 7: John 8–21

Past the seven days here are two options to continue your training. Static Jedis read and re-read the gospels. I suggest other parts of God's Word are equally important, but start with the foundation of ingesting the teachings and life of Jesus for now. That was my initial challenge to myself, and I now pass the challenge to you.

 Read the Word with the intention to be
changed by it, not to change the pages.
Consume God's Word not to get through it
but so it comes through you.
#staticjedi @ericsamueltimm

I read them through in different translations. I like many translations, but one I use quite a bit in exploration and memorization is the more aggressive English Standard Version. The NIV is great and widely used as well. (We can argue all day long on what translation we should be reading, but let's not.) A *parallel* Bible, on the other hand, contains between two and four versions side by side as an instructional tool and great middle ground.

Past the seven days reading one Gospel a month starting in January allows us as Static Jedis to read though all four Gospels four times in a year.

Here is what one Gospel each month looks like throughout the year:

January	February
January	**February**
Day 1: Matthew 1	Day 1: Mark 1:1–28
Day 2: Matthew 2	Day 2: Mark 1:29–45
Day 3: Matthew 3	Day 3: Mark 2:1–17
Day 4: Matthew 4	Day 4: Mark 2:18–28
Day 5: Matthew 5	Day 5: Mark 3
Day 6: Matthew 6	Day 6: Mark 4:1–25
Day 7: Matthew 7	Day 7: Mark 4:26–41
Day 8: Matthew 8	Day 8: Mark 5:1–20
Day 9: Matthew 9	Day 9: Mark 5:21–43
Day 10: Matthew 10	Day 10: Mark 6:1–29
Day 11: Matthew 11	Day 11: Mark 6:30–56
Day 12: Matthew 12	Day 12: Mark 7:1–30
Day 13: Matthew 13	Day 13: Mark 7:31–37
Day 14: Matthew 14	Day 14: Mark 8:1–21
Day 15: Matthew 15	Day 15: Mark 8:22–38
Day 16: Matthew 16	Day 16: Mark 9:1–32
Day 17: Matthew 17	Day 17: Mark 9:33–50
Day 18: Matthew 18	Day 18: Mark 10
Day 19: Matthew 19	Day 19: Mark 11:1–19
Day 20: Matthew 20	Day 20: Mark 11:20–33
Day 21: Matthew 21	Day 21: Mark 12:1–27
Day 22: Matthew 22	Day 22: Mark 12:28–44
Day 23: Matthew 23	Day 23: Mark 13:1–31
Day 24: Matthew 24	Day 24: Mark 13:32–37
Day 25: Matthew 25	Day 25: Mark 14
Day 26: Matthew 26:1–30	Day 26: Mark 15:1–32
Day 27: Matthew 26:31–75	Day 27: Mark 15:33–47
Day 28: Matthew 27:1–31	Day 28: Mark 16
Day 29: Matthew 27:32–66	
Day 30: Matthew 28	
Day 31: Catch up or review	

March

Day 1: Luke 1:1–45
Day 2: Luke 1:46–80
Day 3: Luke 2
Day 4: Luke 3
Day 5: Luke 4:1–30
Day 6: Luke 4:31–44
Day 7: Luke 5
Day 8: Luke 6:1–26
Day 9: Luke 6:27–49
Day 10: Luke 7:1–17
Day 11: Luke 7:18–50
Day 12: Luke 8:1–25
Day 13: Luke 8:26–56
Day 14: Luke 9:1–36
Day 15: Luke 9:37–62
Day 16: Luke 10
Day 17: Luke 11:1–28
Day 18: Luke 11:29–54
Day 19: Luke 12
Day 20: Luke 13
Day 21: Luke 14
Day 22: Luke 15
Day 23: Luke 16
Day 24: Luke 17
Day 25: Luke 18
Day 26: Luke 19
Day 27: Luke 20
Day 28: Luke 21
Day 29: Luke 22
Day 30: Luke 23
Day 31: Luke 24

April

Day 1: John 1:1–34
Day 2: John 1:35–51
Day 3: John 2:1–12
Day 4: John 2:13–25
Day 5: John 3:1–21
Day 6: John 3:22–36
Day 7: John 4:1–38
Day 8: John 4:39–54
Day 9: John 5
Day 10: John 6:1–24
Day 11: John 6:25–71
Day 12: John 7:1–24
Day 13: John 7:25–52
Day 14: John 8:1–30
Day 15: John 8:31–59
Day 16: John 9
Day 17: John 10
Day 18: John 11:1–37
Day 19: John 11:38–57
Day 20: John 12:1–36
Day 21: John 12:37–50
Day 22: John 13
Day 23: John 14
Day 24: John 15
Day 25: John 16
Day 26: John 17
Day 27: John 18
Day 28: John 19
Day 29: John 20
Day 30: John 21

May	**June**
Day 1: Matthew 1	Day 1: Mark 1:1–28
Day 2: Matthew 2	Day 2: Mark 1:29–45
Day 3: Matthew 3	Day 3: Mark 2:1–17
Day 4: Matthew 4	Day 4: Mark 2:18–28
Day 5: Matthew 5	Day 5: Mark 3
Day 6: Matthew 6	Day 6: Mark 4:1–25
Day 7: Matthew 7	Day 7: Mark 4:26–41
Day 8: Matthew 8	Day 8: Mark 5:1–20
Day 9: Matthew 9	Day 9: Mark 5:21–43
Day 10: Matthew 10	Day 10: Mark 6:1–29
Day 11: Matthew 11	Day 11: Mark 6:30–56
Day 12: Matthew 12	Day 12: Mark 7:1–30
Day 13: Matthew 13	Day 13: Mark 7:31–37
Day 14: Matthew 14	Day 14: Mark 8:1–21
Day 15: Matthew 15	Day 15: Mark 8:22–38
Day 16: Matthew 16	Day 16: Mark 9:1–32
Day 17: Matthew 17	Day 17: Mark 9:33–50
Day 18: Matthew 18	Day 18: Mark 10:1–31
Day 19: Matthew 19	Day 19: Mark 10:32–52
Day 20: Matthew 20	Day 20: Mark 11:1–19
Day 21: Matthew 21	Day 21: Mark 11:20–33
Day 22: Matthew 22	Day 22: Mark 12:1–27
Day 23: Matthew 23	Day 23: Mark 12:28–44
Day 24: Matthew 24	Day 24: Mark 13:1–31
Day 25: Matthew 25:1–30	Day 25: Mark 13:32–37
Day 26: Matthew 25:31–46	Day 26: Mark 14:1–42
Day 27: Matthew 26:1–30	Day 27: Mark 14:43–72
Day 28: Matthew 26:31–75	Day 28: Mark 15:1–32
Day 29: Matthew 27:1–31	Day 29: Mark 15:33–47
Day 30: Matthew 27:32–66	Day 30: Mark 16
Day 31 Matthew 28	

July	**August**
Day 1: Luke 1:1–45	Day 1: John 1:1–34
Day 2: Luke 1:46–80	Day 2: John 1:35–51
Day 3: Luke 2	Day 3: John 2:1–12
Day 4: Luke 3	Day 4: John 2:13–25
Day 5: Luke 4:1–30	Day 5: John 3:1–21
Day 6: Luke 4:31–44	Day 6: John 3:22–36
Day 7: Luke 5	Day 7: John 4:1–38
Day 8: Luke 6:1–26	Day 8: John 4:39–54
Day 9: Luke 6:27–49	Day 9: John 5
Day 10: Luke 7:1–17	Day 10: John 6:1–24
Day 11: Luke 7:18–50	Day 11: John 6:25–71
Day 12: Luke 8:1–25	Day 12: John 7:1–24
Day 13: Luke 8:26–56	Day 13: John 7:25–52
Day 14: Luke 9:1–36	Day 14: John 8:1–30
Day 15: Luke 9:37–62	Day 15: John 8:31–59
Day 16: Luke 10	Day 16: John 9
Day 17: Luke 11:1–28	Day 17: John 10
Day 18: Luke 11:29–54	Day 18: John 11:1–37
Day 19: Luke 12	Day 19: John 11:38–57
Day 20: Luke 13	Day 20: John 12:1–36
Day 21: Luke 14	Day 21: John 12:37–50
Day 22: Luke 15	Day 22: John 13
Day 23: Luke 16	Day 23: John 14
Day 24: Luke 17	Day 24: John 15
Day 25: Luke 18	Day 25: John 16
Day 26: Luke 19	Day 26: John 17
Day 27: Luke 20	Day 27: John 18:1–24
Day 28: Luke 21	Day 28: John 18:25–40
Day 29: Luke 22	Day 29: John 19
Day 30: Luke 23	Day 30: John 20
Day 31: Luke 24	Day 31: John 21

September	**October**
Day 1: Matthew 1	Day 1: Mark 1:1–28
Day 2: Matthew 2	Day 2: Mark 1:29–45
Day 3: Matthew 3	Day 3: Mark 2:1–17
Day 4: Matthew 4	Day 4: Mark 2:18–28
Day 5: Matthew 5	Day 5: Mark 3:1–19
Day 6: Matthew 6	Day 6: Mark 3:20–35
Day 7: Matthew 7	Day 7: Mark 4:1–25
Day 8: Matthew 8	Day 8: Mark 4:26–41
Day 9: Matthew 9	Day 9: Mark 5:1–20
Day 10: Matthew 10	Day 10: Mark 5:21–43
Day 11: Matthew 11	Day 11: Mark 6:1–29
Day 12: Matthew 12	Day 12: Mark 6:30–56
Day 13: Matthew 13	Day 13: Mark 7:1–30
Day 14: Matthew 14	Day 14: Mark 7:31–37
Day 15: Matthew 15	Day 15: Mark 8:1–21
Day 16: Matthew 16	Day 16: Mark 8:22–38
Day 17: Matthew 17	Day 17: Mark 9:1–32
Day 18: Matthew 18	Day 18: Mark 9:33–50
Day 19: Matthew 19	Day 19: Mark 10:1–31
Day 20: Matthew 20	Day 20: Mark 10:32–52
Day 21: Matthew 21	Day 21: Mark 11:1–19
Day 22: Matthew 22	Day 22: Mark 11:20–33
Day 23: Matthew 23	Day 23: Mark 12:1–27
Day 24: Matthew 24	Day 24: Mark 12:28–44
Day 25: Matthew 25	Day 25: Mark 13:1–31
Day 26: Matthew 26:1–30	Day 26: Mark 13:32–37
Day 27: Matthew 26:31–75	Day 27: Mark 14:1–42
Day 28: Matthew 27:1–31	Day 28: Mark 14:43–72
Day 29: Matthew 27:32–66	Day 29: Mark 15:1–32
Day 30: Matthew 28	Day 30: Mark 15:33–47
	Day 31: Mark 16

November

Day 1: Luke 1:1–45
Day 2: Luke 1:46–80
Day 3: Luke 2
Day 4: Luke 3
Day 5: Luke 4:1–30
Day 6: Luke 4:31–44
Day 7: Luke 5
Day 8: Luke 6:1–26
Day 9: Luke 6:27–49
Day 10: Luke 7:1–17
Day 11: Luke 7:18–50
Day 12: Luke 8:1–25
Day 13: Luke 8:26–56
Day 14: Luke 9:1–36
Day 15: Luke 9:37–62
Day 16: Luke 10
Day 17: Luke 11
Day 18: Luke 12
Day 19: Luke 13
Day 20: Luke 14
Day 21: Luke 15
Day 22: Luke 16
Day 23: Luke 17
Day 24: Luke 18
Day 25: Luke 19
Day 26: Luke 20
Day 27: Luke 21
Day 28: Luke 22
Day 29: Luke 23
Day 30: Luke 24

December

Day 1: John 1:1–34
Day 2: John 1:35–51
Day 3: John 2:1–12
Day 4: John 2:13–25
Day 5: John 3:1–21
Day 6: John 3:22–36
Day 7: John 4:1–38
Day 8: John 4:39–54
Day 9: John 5
Day 10: John 6:1–24
Day 11: John 6:25–71
Day 12: John 7:1–24
Day 13: John 7:25–52
Day 14: John 8:1–30
Day 15: John 8:31–59
Day 16: John 9
Day 17: John 10
Day 18: John 11:1–37
Day 19: John 11:38–57
Day 20: John 12:1–36
Day 21: John 12:37–50
Day 22: John 13
Day 23: John 14
Day 24: John 15
Day 25: John 16
Day 26: John 17
Day 27: John 18:1–24
Day 28: John 18:25–40
Day 29: John 19
Day 30: John 20
Day 31: John 21

Possibly more time-consuming is reading through all four Gospels each month. With this plan—and you need a plan—the Static Jedi journeys through the Gospels twelve times each year. Here is what that would look like broken down into specific 28-, 30-, and 31-day months:

30-Day Month

Day 1: Matthew 1–5
Day 2: Matthew 6–8
Day 3: Matthew 9–12
Day 4: Matthew 13–14
Day 5: Matthew 15–18
Day 6: Matthew 19–21
Day 7: Matthew 22–24
Day 8: Matthew 25–26
Day 9: Matthew 27–28
Day 10: Mark 1–4
Day 11: Mark 5–8
Day 12: Mark 9–10
Day 13: Mark 11–13
Day 14: Mark 14–16
Day 15: Luke 1–2
Day 16: Luke 3–5
Day 17: Luke 6–7
Day 18: Luke 8–9
Day 19: Luke 10–12
Day 20: Luke 13–15
Day 21: Luke 16–18
Day 22: Luke 19–21
Day 23: Luke 22–23
Day 24: Luke 24–John 3
Day 25: John 4–5
Day 26: John 6–8
Day 27: John 9–11
Day 28: John 12–14
Day 29: John 15–18
Day 30: John 19–21

31-Day Month

Day 1: Matthew 1–3
Day 2: Matthew 4–7
Day 3: Matthew 8–9
Day 4: Matthew 10–12
Day 5: Matthew 13–14
Day 6: Matthew 15–18
Day 7: Matthew 19–21
Day 8: Matthew 22–24
Day 9: Matthew 25–26
Day 10: Matthew 27–28
Day 11: Mark 1–4
Day 12: Mark 5–8
Day 13: Mark 9–10
Day 14: Mark 11–13
Day 15: Mark 14–16
Day 16: Luke 1–2
Day 17: Luke 3–5
Day 18: Luke 6–7
Day 19: Luke 8–9
Day 20: Luke 10–12
Day 21: Luke 13–15
Day 22: Luke 16–18
Day 23: Luke 19–21
Day 24: Luke 22–23
Day 25: Luke 24–John 3
Day 26: John 4–5
Day 27: John 6–8
Day 28: John 9–11
Day 29: John 12–14
Day 30: John 15–18
Day 31: John 19–21

28-Day Month

Day 1: Matthew 1–5
Day 2: Matthew 6–8
Day 3: Matthew 9–12
Day 4: Matthew 13–14
Day 5: Matthew 15–18
Day 6: Matthew 19–21
Day 7: Matthew 22–24
Day 8: Matthew 25–26
Day 9: Matthew 27–28
Day 10: Mark 1–4
Day 11: Mark 5–8
Day 12: Mark 9–10
Day 13: Mark 11–13
Day 14: Mark 14–16
Day 15: Luke 1–3
Day 16: Luke 4–6
Day 17: Luke 7–9
Day 18: Luke 10–12
Day 19: Luke 13–15
Day 20: Luke 16–18
Day 21: Luke 19–21
Day 22: Luke 22–23
Day 23: Luke 24–John 3
Day 24: John 4–5
Day 25: John 6–8
Day 26: John 9–11
Day 27: John 12–16
Day 28: John 17–21

We journey to become a Static Master by reading Jesus's teachings found in the Gospels and becoming more and more familiar with God's Word. To know Jesus is to know the Word.

> And the Word became flesh and dwelt among us, and we have seen his glory, glory as of the only Son from the Father, full of grace and truth.
>
> —JOHN 1:14

Jesus asks us to abide, remain, tarry, continue in, be present to, be held, hold, and kept in His Word—and if we do as He asks, we are truly His disciples.

> If you abide in my word, you are truly my disciples.
>
> —JOHN 8:31

Let the Word sink into your flesh.

Abide in it, to the point of memorization.

Set a goal to memorize a chapter of Matthew. Or maybe the whole book.

I have set an extended goal for myself, not because it's something I have to do to earn salvation, but because it's something I *get* to do to know Jesus more.

My goal is to memorize the entire Book of Matthew.

And I will memorize the Book of Matthew by memorizing one verse at a time.

If you want to join me, this means that for 1,070 verses in Matthew, we need to memorize three verses a week. This will take about seven years.

It can be done.

Seven years is a short time, really, when compared to the rest of your life.

For this to happen, I'm going to have work on memorization before I check Facebook.

You and I will forever be chained to the noise

if we check Facebook

or consume the noise

before reading God's Word.

Ask yourself every day before you check into the noise, "Did I read God's Word?"

If the answer is no, then your next action is to read the Bible. Make it a habit to reach for the Bible before reaching for social media, the phone, breakfast, or anything else. Time with the Lord in His Word should be priority one every day.

We live out of order and wonder why we can obtain no sense of order.

If you have invested the firstfruits of your day to Jesus, then by all means update away

—and say hi at facebook.com/ericsamueltimm

or follow me at twitter.com/ericsamueltimm.

Or send me a pic on Instagram: @ericsamueltimm.

We could talk about this book you're reading.

But beware the trap of reading books about the Book before you read the Bible. Start each study book from the foundation of the raw Word of God. From this perspective books come alive and a deeper understanding grows. Without this foundation the other books can become mere information that slides over the surface of our being. God's Word, on the other hand, deeply impacts us.

Would you rather someone asked others about you or that they come to know you directly? That's how it is with Scripture and the Word of God—through God's Word, we come to know Him directly.

Scripture cuts us to our bone marrow. Hebrews 4:12 describes Scripture as "living and active, sharper than any two-edged sword, piercing to the division of soul and of spirit, of joints and of marrow, and discerning the thoughts and intentions of the heart."

Other books you read about the Book, or possibly for entertainment purposes, have their place. You read them with a sense of interpreting them, considering what is being said as they only yield a single sharp edge.

The Bible, though, is not meant to be just considered.
It is meant to be lived out
in real life
and obeyed.
Unlike other books
the Word interprets the reader
and directly cuts,
like a doubled-edged sword,
deep into our being.
So make the sword ready.
Know your weapon well.

A Static Jedi seeks Jesus in God's Word with an intent to memorize it. Incorporating Scripture memory into the journey of your life makes God's Word a guiding force in your heart. Seek it to the point of earthly hunger. A Static Jedi develops a hunger for the bread found in the Word of God that's greater than a hunger for the bread of this earth.

Will you hunger for this more than food?

■ INTERNAL INQUIRY ■

1. Is it possible for you to read the Gospels through each month or year?

2. How will you set yourself up to do this?

3. What is your goal for memorizing portions of the Bible?

■ EXTERNAL EXCHANGE ■

1. Has the Bible ever spoken to you? What was the revelation you received?

2. What goal have you fallen short of before? Why did you fail? What do you want to do differently this time?

3. What is the importance of having a plan and a goal, rather than just seeing what happens?

Chapter 16

HUNGRY COPY MACHINES

FINALLY WE JOURNEY to skillfully and intentionally apply the final two keys Jesus gives us to live out this mastery of noise in our lives according to His example.

KEY #4: A Fasting Life

Fasting is different from consecration, using a biblical definition. Consecration means being set apart for a certain use, to purify something for a specific purpose. Fasting, on the other hand, is about going without food for a spiritual purpose. Don't confuse fasting food with withdrawing from Facebook or movies or other kinds of noise—those aren't the same as fasting.

One of my favorite things to consecrate is the day to my family. My family, my first ministry, has what we call "analog day" most weeks. These are days we shut off all phones and electronics and choose to rest in a true Sabbath. It's a day of rest and interacting with one another. We eat, laugh, and get intense—as intense as you can get over a few games of Hungry Hippos. (Sidenote: Electric ukuleles are allowed.)

That time is consecrated, not fasted.

Do you see the difference?

In God's Word fasting involves food. If it doesn't involve food, then it's not fasting. Some would argue that you can fast TV, movies, video games, and other nonfood items. I say items you can set aside for the rest of your life and still live are consecrated, not fasted.

One item you cannot set aside for the rest of your life is food. Food is fuel for the body. Unless there is some intervention of God, without food we would die. I want to be clear, then, in my best yet feeble attempt to stick to Scripture about what fasting is and isn't, since a Static Jedi does both—consecration and fasting. It has helped me to know the difference.

 In God's Word fasting involves food. If it doesn't involve food, then it's not fasting. #staticjedi @ericsamueltimm

This discipline of fasting is one of deep importance and is a private practice for the Static Jedi. It's a practice found before and after the cross of Christ. Moses fasted when he received God's law (Deut. 9:9). Paul fasted while he was in danger (Acts 27:33–36). And as we've already covered, Jesus began His ministry with fasting.

We should just begin.

Begin seeing this key for what it is: powerful.

Jesus displays this power in Matthew 17. Here the disciples can't remove a demon from a boy. But Jesus removes the stronghold and the disciples can't figure out why they were ineffective. After all, if you flip back in your Bible to Matthew 10, you see Jesus give them the power to do these things. Why couldn't they expel the evil spirit out of this boy? He responded that some fights with the enemy are only won with "prayer and fasting."

We need more than just prayer in our lives, in other words.

But there are different types of fasting. Which one was Jesus talking about? Possibly all of them or possibly one. Either way, let's look at the three different types of fasts.

I have been helped by a few resources to know the differences between fasts from the biblical perspective, in order to avoid defeat. One resource is an old book from 1940 by Reverend Franklin Hall titled *Atomic Power With God Through Fasting and Prayer*. It's more like a brochure, but I appreciate the old books. They are what the new books are birthed from. More readily available and equally powerful is the work of Pastor Jentezen Franklin in a book called *Fasting*. Both books explore fasting in depth; however, Pastor Franklin speaks in the heavier prose of our time.

You will find three kinds of fasts mentioned in Scripture and covered in these resources:

1. The absolute fast. I would never personally recommend or endorse this extreme fast. This is a fast where you take in no food and no water. I wouldn't even think about attempting it.

2. The normal fast. This fast includes water—and a lot of it. However, it excludes food. There are some variations on longer fasts that allow you to consume broth or juice.

3. The Daniel fast. In the Book of Daniel we see him fasting in such a way that he took nothing pleasurable from the king's table—no meat, no wine, no breads, and no sweets, plus a few other omitted items. In its basic form, if it can produce a seed, you can eat it during a Daniel fast. Susan Gregory's *The Daniel Fast* is a helpful book for exploring this option.

It's worth knowing that Daniel fasted for twenty-one days and then an angel appeared and spoke to him about the mysteries concerning the issues at hand. We read these stories of the supernatural, and we react typically: "What a powerful story!"

But we are going to further that reaction into action. We're going to help our response become one that says, "What a powerful story *that I can live!*"

That "then" can be now! Daniel didn't read the Bible backward like we do, but he did fast. We can see the supernatural, but is it possible we miss it because we don't do the natural? Could it be we can't see it because we fail to fast? A Spirit-led life leads to fasting. Walking by the Spirit leads us to and through the events found in the Book of Daniel.

For the next seven days, then, I challenge you to fast one meal per day or possibly one full day. Maybe you have never done this before. Great! Maybe you have done it before. Great for you too.

If you need to consult your doctor, do so. Then pick a meal other than breakfast to fast every day for a week, or choose one full day of the week to fast, and fast by way of the normal fast or the way Daniel did for it. Both types of fast include a lot of water.

Once you get past the seven days, I suggest you fast at least once a year on the Daniel fast or the normal fast. The length is up to you. I can only reveal, not for public attention but for teaching purposes, what has practically worked for me and others. One approach is to fast the first seven days of January and then the first three days of each month of the year with the Daniel fast or the normal fast. This adds up to forty days total in a calendar year of committing to bring death to the flesh through a fast. It allows you to give God the first days of the year and the first days of each month, and God appreciates firsts—firstfruits, first loves, first sons, first offspring, first hours of a day, and first thoughts. After the Hebrews' seven-day silence, Joshua stormed the city of Jericho, and it was the first of many cities conquered. Jericho's firstfruits were offered to God according to His request and to honor God for His provision.

Jesus also fasted for forty days to begin His ministry. I can certainly fast forty days a year to continue my own ministry, as I believe followers of Christ, the Static Master, are to do.

Here are a few items to remember in this process:

1. Fast privately. In Matthew 6 Jesus addresses the dangers of public declarations of the spiritual merit badge.

2. Use the time you would be eating to withdraw and seek God. If you are not using the time to seek God, you are not fasting. You are dieting.

3. Start slowly and in line with your physical condition. It's not easy to fast, and that's the point.

Fasting is about seeking the bread from heaven more than the bread of this earth.

Jesus's words echo in my heart as He says, "Take, eat this bread which is broken for you." He says take and eat, but we still choose to eat. What are you eating? Break the chains of earthly bread to find the noise beneath you as you search for the bread from heaven.

Choose the way of the master of the static. Fast.

KEY #5: Choose to Create Disciples, Then Do So

Discipleship is duplication. There are a few practices that help this process once the choice is made. In no way is this section an exhaustive study of what discipleship, community, and living life together with Jesus looks like. However, here are a few keys that I have intentionally integrated in those that I disciple that create a great foundation to grow from. I'll point them out.

The disciples and Jesus invested time together.

In Acts we see the early church gathered together, breaking bread, taking journeys, and going out in service with one another many times. Moments filled with rest, meals, teaching, and ministry all have the common denominator of time invested together. This is the rich community we create with others.

Investing time with your disciples—your life community—is important.

The disciples and Jesus prayed together.

Sometimes while praying and seeking God together, the disciples were caught sleeping. Busted! Jesus asked His disciples to pray with Him in Matthew 26. Even the early church, in Acts, we see the believers practiced prayer together as a part of the time they invested in each other.

Praying with your disciples—your life community—is important.

The disciples where shaped by Jesus's words, which is the Word.

Jesus asked His disciples and us to be shaped by the Word and devoted to truth. John 8:31–32 says "If you abide in my word, you are truly my disciples, and you will know the truth, and the truth will set you free." Acts 2:42 records, "And they devoted themselves to the apostles' teaching and the fellowship, to the breaking of bread and the prayers."

The study and application of the Word with your disciples—your life community—is important.

The disciples shared times of rest and meals with Jesus.

The breaking of bread is a pivotal part of the holy moment at the Lord's Supper when Jesus established communion: "Now as they were eating, Jesus took bread, and after blessing it broke it and gave it to the disciples, and said, "Take, eat; this is my body" (Matt. 26:26). Similarly the early church gathered together often in fellowship and the breaking of bread in each other's homes.

Eating and having communion with your disciples—your life community—is important.

The disciples were with Jesus during many intense ministry moments.

At specific locations during His ministry Jesus went out and fed, served, healed, taught, and loved people. The disciples had a front-row, hands-on experience at many of the events. In the early church, in Acts, these first disciples went together into the streets, to prisons, and on missionary journeys.

Serving the community in ministry with your disciples—your life community—is important.

This investment of time, commitment to prayer, and study of the Word launched from places of rest, meals, and conversation with your disciples will lead you to seeing lives changed by the power of the gospel. Static Jedis disciple as the Static Master did, becoming a student in the art of this discipleship process. Teaching others what we have mastered, or are attempting to master, is the way of discipleship. Discipleship through duplication is Jesus's example.

Our master teacher, Jesus, invites us as His students, His servants, to be like Him:

> A disciple is not above his teacher, nor a servant above his master. It is enough for the disciple to be like his teacher, and the servant like his master.
> —MATTHEW 10:24–25

Paul implores, "Be imitators of me, as I am of Christ" (1 Cor. 11:1).

Take the pressure off. Maybe it's not twelve people you disciple at one time.

Put the pressure back on. Maybe your number is currently zero.

To make disciples, we must choose them. What would be your answer if anyone asked you right now, "Who are you discipling?" If you can't directly point to your disciples, you are missing the last key to becoming a Static Jedi. In this process our newly acquired information becomes seated in our hearts, and we impart the knowledge of God found within this place, not just in our heads. The noise is continually mastered when we teach and instruct others in what we know and learn. It gives us a chance to live out what Jesus asked us to do in community.

Who are you personally discipling?

If you're married, your spouse could be on your list. If you're a parent, your children certainly are on it. If you are a grandparent, your grandchildren or students in the youth group at your church possibly would be on your list. (As a side note, grandparents are perfectly suited to teach the children's and teen programs at church. Let the younger generation learn from the mature members of the church and community while the young parents who are busy all week with child rearing sit in church and Sunday school for an hour or two to be spiritually fed!) If you are a pastor, your entire church is *not* on this list. Who are your twelve—or two or three—that you're discipling as Jesus modeled?

Without Jesus selecting the Twelve, things would have looked much different than they do now. He trained that handful of ruffians who changed the world. Imagine trusting a dozen guys who were not the elite of their era to be the ones to carry the gospel to the world. Think of it. You're holding this book because there were disciples.

Likewise, a Static Jedi will change the world by changing someone else's world.

Jesus made the choice to make disciples—to choose the Twelve. So you too must choose to purposefully integrate this discipline into your life.

It's not an easy task.

However, let me be clear, like clean water: having people in your life whom you are discipling while you too remain a disciple must be a priority equal in importance to drinking water. It's necessary for life.

You may have a list of excuses.

"I'm not an expert on water chemistry."

"I do not have a degree in water."

"I don't fully understand the theology behind ice, gas, and liquid forms of water."

"I can't swim."

"I can't ski."

"I've never dug a well."

"The water I knew was different."

"I drink too much pop, soda, and Coke."

Whatever your excuse, it easily falls to the wayside, as we all know we need water. So we seek it. Seek your disciples, for you have found the living water.

For the next seven days prayerfully examine your plan for discipleship and consider who you are tangibly discipling. Ask God to direct you, just as He did Jesus, to the right people for the right time.

After those seven days of prayer I would extend the challenge for you to continue to grow in the art of discipleship. I would suggest going through this book with your life community, small group, disciples, youth group, and maybe your entire church. After that launch into the deeper understanding outlined in the five keys of our quest for mastery.

The following are books I continue to read in my quest to become a better disciple maker. They have helped me pencil in a picture found in the ink of the pages of the Word. They are good to study in tandem with the Word itself.

1. *The Cost of Discipleship* and *Life Together* by Dietrich Bonhoeffer

2. *Radical* and *Radical Together* by David Platt

3. *Crazy Love* and *Multiply* by Francis Chan

4. *The Pursuit of God* and *The Knowledge of the Holy* by A.W. Tozer

The Static Master chose disciples. The Static Jedi becomes a disciple of the master and then chooses someone, or several someones, to develop into Static Jedis too. That's how Jesus could leave the earth, having entrusted His world-changing, eternity-affecting message with twelve followers. They were His disciples sent on a quest to be the Static Jedis of their day and duplicate themselves.

Will you join them?

■ INTERNAL INQUIRY ■

1. Are there any reasons you don't you want to fast?

2. Do you have disciples? If not, what's holding you back?

3. How can you help your church look more like the church found in Acts?

■ EXTERNAL EXCHANGE ■

1. How can we learn more together about becoming disciples?

2. Is a disciple the same as a Christian? How might they be different?

3. What did the early church look like?

Chapter 17

THE END IS THE BEGINNING

GET A CLEAR glass and pour in some water. Fill the glass just a bit over half full, about 60 percent. I'll wait. OK, back with your glass? Now look at it.

Walking Water

If your body was that glass, that is about how much water you are made of right now. Up to 60 percent of your body is water. Your brain is about 70 percent water, and your lungs can be near to 90 percent water. Even your bones are not the dry steel skeleton of a building. Quite the opposite. Your bones are about 22 percent water.

Plainly, you are walking water.

We catch glimpses of water all over this globe, which is around 70 percent covered by water—water frozen in time, rushing rivers, quiet streams, playful or destructive waves, and my personal favorite, water that is still like glass. When water on a lake or in the confines of a harbor has been protected by the elements or the weather is just perfect, water takes on the appearance of a sheet of glass. This is the best time to own and operate a wake board or to just sit and enjoy the art. There is nothing quite like it. This scene captured in creation has sold a lot of postcards. That moment with the sun rising or setting upon the liquid surface with the backdrop of creation creates a surreal, color-rich moment to reflect on life.

While in the course of your reflection you would eventually digress to one of life's basic needs to support life: we must consume water, the very thing we gaze upon.

Water can be still.

Water can be static.

---

static |'statik|

1 lacking in movement, action

2 Physics concerned with bodies at rest or forces in equilibrium.[1]

Water can lack movement and action. A body of water can be at rest with forces in equilibrium. We are water. And the walking water can be still. We too can be static. Internally at rest.

However, much opposition to you finding this rest will continue to arise.

Will you rise above the noise?

There is a constant external static that desires to pull us from being concerned with keeping the soul, spirit, and body at rest. This must concern us and spark us to become Static Jedis, experts in spiritual static. By shielding ourselves from the external forces that challenge our internal spiritual equilibrium—the noise—we find internal equilibrium.

The journey begins and ends with the keys that Jesus, the Static Master, gave us as He lived. Even in times of arguably external imbalance in Jesus's life, we see these keys leading Him back to rest.

Creatures like us, made of this much water, need rest.

Leia and Jedi

Dogs drink a lot of water too or at least attempt to. I'm sure cats also drink water for all you cat people. However, they do not drink water like dogs. Cats are cautious and secret ninja water drinkers. Dogs lap it up loudly and splatter it everywhere. Then it drips from their furry chin for the next ten minutes. This is what happens with my dog, at least. The water shrapnel from her drinking gets so bad in the summer, I have to put two large beach towels on the ground to catch the cascading drips and runoff from her jowls.

My friend's puppy is exactly like this, only smaller. She is a border collie—a herding dog developed in the Anglo-Scottish border region for herding livestock, especially sheep. They named her Leia. Leia would herd her "sheep," otherwise known as the three boys, Fin, Aiden, and Reilly. Leia loves those boys, and they love her. They got Leia recently, but before her they had a male collie, their first love. They named him Jedi. They also love that dog very much.

Once an animal steals our hearts, a strange thing happens. The animal becomes a family member, caught posing in Christmas cards and receiving basic life care in the form of water, food, shelter, and love from its owners. If you have a pet, you love it. The prevailing connection between man and animal is powerfully displayed in our relationships with domestic pets.

Pets possess something else we mark upon them: a name. The name becomes a part of their identity. The name Jedi for my friend's dog, for example, is traced to a group of warriors in George Lucas's epic story *Star Wars*—a must-see classic. Jedi is also a form of the name Jedediah. Hebrew in origin, *Jedediah* means beloved of the Lord, friend of the Lord, friend of God, and the hand.[2]

Let this name, Static Jedi, become a part of your identity. Be named "a body of water at rest, in internal balance, marked as one beloved and known by God, an extension of His hands."

Be named a Static Jedi.

Owning the Name

How does this happen again?

Tear down the wall.

Invest your time wisely and carefully, no matter your past foundation or habits.

Pursue God as a person, and live with your identity found in Christ—you are a son or daughter.

Beware of the false mastery that lies ahead and be challenged by the way Jesus lived.

Grasp and live out the five keys of rising early, withdrawing to pray, memorizing the Word, fasting to rule the flesh, and duplicating disciples to do the same.

From this underpinning the noise becomes our puppet.

 By shielding ourselves from the external forces that challenge our internal spiritual equilibrium—the noise—we find internal equilibrium. #staticjedi @ericsamueltimm

So don't cheapen the past or tomorrow by quitting. Don't give up the sublime opportunity to live closer to God today. God moving in our lives, families, and churches is God staying where He is. We move toward Him and away from the noise.

It's not about what you do; it's about what He's done so we are free to live.

Live to know Jesus.

In Jesus you already *are* a Static Jedi—

No longer weighed by sin,

Internally at rest,

Beloved by God,

By grace through faith.

The two work together—grace and faith—so you don't have to do anything else.

You don't have to earn anything.

The work has been done.

Faith is our response to what Jesus already provided: grace.

> And without faith it is impossible to please him, for whoever would draw near to God must believe that he exists and that he rewards those who seek him.
>
> —HEBREWS 11:6

For those who seek Him—this is a get to.

You get to be one of "those."

The reward is far greater than the noise.

Now choose.

Make the choice to become a Static Jedi.

One who lives no longer weighed down by noise.

Externally in pursuit of God's beloved, Jesus.

Live your life that is lived to the fullest.

Awake to the strings that have held you.

Love the things that eternally hold you.

Think on the things that grow you.

Speak from the depths that will find you.

Master the noise, lest it master you.

> Awake, O sleeper, and arise from the dead, and Christ will shine on you.
>
> —EPHESIANS 5:14

■ INTERNAL INQUIRY ■

1. Since you already are a Static Jedi, why should you continue to become one?

2. How can you invest your time and energy wisely from this point forward, regardless of your past foundations or habits?

3. How will you make the five keys of Jesus's life a part of your own life?

■ EXTERNAL EXCHANGE ■

1. What are the five keys for living out the life of a Static Jedi?

2. How can we make those keys an inward part of who we are?

3. Who needs a copy of this book? Can you give a copy to them?

4. Can your small group or church journey with you in this?

EPILOGUE

A T ONE TIME everything was formless and void. Days pass until breath and dust collide, intentionally. Then there is man with no books, no publishers, no authors, no readers, no pages...

This is the way it was in the beginning.

Trace the roots of Christianity back. The further you go, the more you will discover a people of verbal and oral tradition. The people of God used this once-breathed inward breath to then exhale out God's story. These people—a fundamentally oral Israel—used this same breath to teach and tell stories. Breathing out in story form to the community to form the community.

The community was vital to the story. The story lived on and breathed because people lived and breathed together with the story. The breath was a part of the story.

Then man started to write the breath down. Ink started to replace what was only breath.

This continued until tension surfaced between the authority of a verbal teacher or the distant writer. This tension roared within man: either stay the active listener or become a removed reader. This focus shifted us to reading the breath rather than the physical listening of it.

The progression brought this struggle in man to the place of reading the breath alone, in isolated fashion.

The struggle to pass information or tradition by way of verbal or written tradition is not so much ours today. We have an abundance of information and unlimited accessibility to it.

However, there is an undertow of isolated readers.

This must be bookended by engaged, reading, breathing communities of breath.

In this marvelous replacement this reveals the struggle.

For us the struggle is of the individual or the community.

Books allow us to read alone. This can feed this struggle.

Individuality easily replaces community.

If I may make a plea:

Embrace this struggle with your community.

You may want to reread this book with your tribe.

There is strength in numbers and power in breathing together.

During the transition to a written people, a few thinkers with voices breathed above the noise.

"Written words seem to talk to you as though they were intelligent, but if you ask them anything about what they say, from a desire to be further instructed, they go on telling you the same thing forever."

Socrates said that.

A long time ago.

History does repeat itself.

In this case we are the gatekeeper of this repetition.

This is the time we should revisit this perspective of my mere words on this page.

May the breath of God say to you what you need to read in this book, and may your community of believers help you live what you say.

Breathe together as well as read alone.

NOTES

Chapter 1
Are You a Static Jedi?

1. Associates for Biblical Research, "The Walls of Jericho," http://www.biblearchaeology.org/post/2008/06/the-walls-of -jericho.aspx#Article (accessed April 3, 2013).

2. Blue Letter Bible, "Dictionary and Word Search for *psychē* (Strong's 5590)," http://www.blueletterbible.org/lang/lexicon/ lexicon.cfm?Strongs=G5590&t=KJV (accessed May 9, 2013).

3. C. S. Lewis, *The Screwtape Letters* (New York: Harper-Collins, 2001).

4. ThinkExist.com, "C. S. Lewis Quotes," http://thinkexist .com/quotes/c.s._lewis/ (accessed April 3, 2013).

Chapter 2
Clocks and Cash

1. *Dead Poets Society*, directed by Peter Weir (Burbank, CA: Touchstone Pictures, 1989), DVD.

2. *Merriam-Webster's Collegiate Dictionary*, 11th edition (Springfield, MA: Merriam-Webster, Inc., 2003), s.v. "mastery."

3. Joseph Carroll, "Workers' Average Commute Round-Trip Is 46 Minutes in a Typical Day," http://www.gallup.com/ poll/28504/workers-average-commute-roundtrip-minutes -typical-day.aspx (accessed April 4, 2013).

Chapter 3
Oil and Water

1. Christian Quotes, "Faith Quotes," http://christian-quotes .ochristian.com/Faith-Quotes/ (accessed May 9, 2013).

2. "Are You Washed in the Blood?" by Elisha A. Hoffman. Public domain.

Chapter 4
Just Butter, Baby

1. François de La Rochefoucauld, *Moral Maxims and Reflections* (London: Methuen & Co. Ltd., 1912), http://www.bartleby.com/350/4.html (accessed March 4, 2013).

2. BrainyQuote, http://www.brainyquote.com/quotes/quotes/m/mothertere108724.html (accessed March 4, 2013).

3. ThinkExist.com, "Jim Elliot Quotes," http://thinkexist.com/quotation/he_is_no_fool_who_gives_what_he_cannot_keep_to/193736.html (accessed April 4, 2013).

Chapter 5
Twin Stones to Stand Upon

1. A. W. Tozer, *The Pursuit of God* (Harrisburg, PA: Christian Publications Inc., 1948).

Chapter 6
Pseudo-Static Masters

1. OxfordDictionaries.com, s.v. "pseudo," http://oxforddictionaries.com/es/buscar/english-german/?q=pseudo&multi=1 (accessed April 4, 2013).

Chapter 7
Quasi-Static Masters

1. OxfordDictionaries.com, s.v. "quasi," http://oxforddictionaries.com/us/definition/american_english/quasi- (accessed March 4, 2013).

2. BrainyQuote, http://www.brainyquote.com/quotes/quotes/a/alberteins163057.html (accessed April 5, 2013).

3. Stop Hunger Now, "Hunger Facts," http://www.stophungernow.org/site/PageServer?pagename=learn_facts (accessed April 5, 2013).

4. *Merriam-Webster's Collegiate Dictionary*, s.v. "hallowed."

Chapter 8
Noisy Lives = Noisy Churches = ?

1. BrainyQuote, http://www.brainyquote.com/quotes/quotes/
t/thomasakem108503.html (accessed April 5, 2013).

2. BrainyQuote, http://www.brainyquote.com/quotes/quotes/
l/leotolstoy105644.html (accessed April 5, 2013).

Chapter 9
The Static Master (Part 1):
Jesus Rose Early and Withdrew

1. Henry David Thoreau, *Walden* (Mineola, NY: Dover Publications Inc., 1995).

2. E. M. Bounds, *Power Through Prayer* (Radford, VA: Wilder Publications, 2008).

3. Thomas à Kempis, *The Imitation of Christ* (New York: Vintage Spiritual Classics, 1998).

4. Bounds, *Power Through Prayer.*

5. Ibid.

6. David G. R. Keller, *Isidore of Pelusia Desert Banquet* (Collegeville, MN: Liturgical Press, 2012)/

7. Dietrich Bonhoeffer, *Life Together* (New York: Harper and Row, 1952)

8. à Kempis, *The Imitation of Christ.*

Chapter 10
The Static Master (Part 2):
Jesus Memorized God's Word

1. Dallas Willard, *The Great Omission* (New York: HarperCollins Publishers, 2006), 58. Viewed at Google Books.

Chapter 11
The Static Master (Part 3):
Jesus Fasted and Discipled

1. Richard E Byrd, *Alone: The Classic Polar Adventure* (Washington, DC: Island Press, 2003), 120.

2. Goodreads.com, "Frederick Douglass Quotes," http://www
.goodreads.com/quotes/118842-without-a-struggle-there-can-be
-no-progress (accessed April 11, 2013).

3. As quoted in Bounds, *Power Through Prayer*.

4. *Jerry Maguire*, directed by Cameron Crowe (Culver City,
CA: Sony Pictures Home Entertainment, 1996), DVD.

Chapter 12
New Beginning

1. ThinkExist.com, "Nelson Mandela Quotes," http://
thinkexist.com/quotation/it-always-seems-impossible-until-its
-done/357018.html (accessed April 11, 2013).

2. Goodreads.com, "Dietrich Bonhoeffer Quotes," http://
www.goodreads.com/quotes/264401-action-springs-not-from
-thought-but-from-a-readiness-for (accessed May 9, 2013).

Chapter 13
Green Men Speak Truth

1. Biblestudytools.com, s.v. "qadash," http://www
.biblestudytools.com/lexicons/hebrew/nas/qadash.html (accessed
April 11, 2013).

2. As quoted in Malcolm Muggeridge, *Something Beautiful
for God* (New York: Harper & Row, 1986), 66.

Chapter 14
Early Arts of Drawing and Prayer

1. T. S. Eliot, *Ash Wednesday* (London, Faber & Faber, 1933).

2. Andrew Wommack, *A Better Way to Pray* (Tulsa, OK:
Harrison House Publishers, 2007)

3. Richard J. Foster, *Celebration of Discipline* (New York:
Harper Collins, 2009), 97.

Chapter 15
Swords in Hotel Drawers

1. Goodreads.com, "James Emery White Quotes," http://
www.goodreads.com/author/quotes/123352.James_Emery_White
(accessed May 9, 2013).

Chapter 17
The End Is the Beginning

1. OxfordDictionaries.com, s.v. "static," http:// oxforddictionaries.com/us/definition/american_english/static (accessed April 12, 2013).

2. Sheknows.com, "Jedidiah," http://www.sheknows.com/ baby-names/name/jedidiah (accessed June 18, 2013); Wikipedia, "Jedediah," http://en.wikipedia.org/wiki/Jedediah (accessed June 18, 2013).

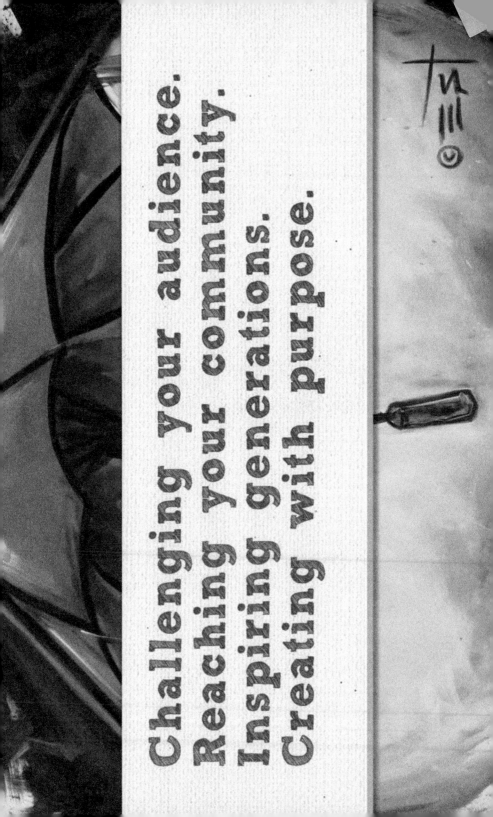

Challenging your audience.
Reaching your community.
Inspiring generations.
Creating with purpose.

Eric Samuel Timm

artist. author. communicator. netflix subscriber.

Inquire to have Eric Samuel Timm communicate at your church or event. Use the contact information found on NoOneUnderground.com.

To purchase Eric's Art and Ministry Resources please visit NOUstore.com.

Find Eric on Facebook, Twitter, and Instagram @ericsamueltimm.

FREE NEWSLETTERS
TO HELP EMPOWER YOUR LIFE

Why subscribe today?

❑ **DELIVERED DIRECTLY TO YOU.** All you have to do is open your inbox and read.

❑ **EXCLUSIVE CONTENT.** We cover the news overlooked by the mainstream press.

❑ **STAY CURRENT.** Find the latest court rulings, revivals, and cultural trends.

❑ **UPDATE OTHERS.** Easy to forward to friends and family with the click of your mouse.

CHOOSE THE E-NEWSLETTER THAT INTERESTS YOU MOST:

- Christian news
- Daily devotionals
- Spiritual empowerment
- And much, much more

SIGN UP AT: **http://freenewsletters.charismamag.com**

8178